# Hudson River Steamboat Catastrophes

# HUDSON RIVER STEAMBOAT

## CATASTROPHES

⇜ CONTESTS & COLLISIONS ⇝

J. Thomas Allison

THE
History
PRESS

Published by The History Press
Charleston, SC 29403
www.historypress.net

First published 2013

ISBN 978-1-5402-2207-7

Library of Congress CIP data applied for.

*For John Blakely Cross (1935–1989), who was the inspiration.*

*If History were taught in the form of stories, it would never be forgotten.*
*—Rudyard Kipling (1865–1936)*

*The only thing new in the world is the History you don't know.*
*—President Harry S. Truman (1884–1972)*

*Words are written in color, not black and white.*
*—Madeleine L'Engle (1918–2007)*

# CONTENTS

# ACKNOWLEDGEMENTS

Locating original source material is difficult. It requires the help of professionals with an intimate knowledge of the archived resources in their care. The Capital District has some of the best collections of historical materials, and I am grateful to the individuals who helped provide access. The Albany Institute of History and Art, with the assistance of Tammis Groft, Allison Munsell and Dr. Douglas McCombs, provided a wealth of photographs that tell the story as clearly as any accomplished author. The Columbia County Historical Society and Diane Shewchuck helped with steamboat artifacts. In the Pruyn Room of the Albany Library, city historian Tony Opalka has been generous with his time and his extensive knowledge of the riverfront. The Rensselaer County Historical Society and county historian Kathryn Sheehan have provided information not found in Albany about steamboats in the region. The librarians and assistants in the New York State Archives made it possible to mine the wealth that has been preserved there for our use. Digital research has come of age. The greatest resource for me was the website "Old Fulton Post Cards," managed and updated by Tom Trynski.

I appreciate the direction, suggestions, answers to my questions and plain listening from some longtime friends and friends I have made while writing this book: the late Florence Christoph, who was the Schuyler family genealogist; Danielle Cherniak; Ann and Donald Eberle; Helen Hill; Paul Dunleavy; John Mickelbank; Richard Becker; Harry Olynx; and Margaret Sullivan.

# ACKNOWLEDGEMENTS

Particularly with a first-time author, the book only becomes a reality with the staff of a good publishing house, such as The History Press. One has a multitude of questions, the need for selective guidance and the insecurities involved in getting it right. The commissioning editor has to be a special person, and for me, that has been Whitney Tarella Landis.

# INTRODUCTION

Albany's shoreline today is a sleepy stretch of the Hudson River with a park, the World War II destroyer escort the USS *Slater* and an excursion boat. On August 17, 1807, portrait painter turned engineer and inventor Robert Fulton began the first scheduled steamboat service between New York and Albany. It took thirty-two hours to cover the 150 miles with one overnight stop. The belching smoke, sparks, noise and splashing paddles of the early boats were compared to the devil sailing a gristmill up the river.

Travel was only possible between late March and early December, when the river was ice free and open to navigation. The public loved skimming along at the breathtaking speed of ten miles an hour while the big wooden wheels churned the Hudson. In the late 1820s, 150 people at a time spent eighteen hours on a steamboat rather than four days in a stagecoach or on a sloop. By midcentury, nearly 1,000 at a time were making the trip in less than eight hours. In the height of summer aboard one of four steamers, another 500 to 800 could experience a night in the luxury reserved for the rich on land. On the river, it was all theirs for the price of the ticket.

Today, a few lithographs by Currier and Ives and oil paintings of a few boats appear to be what is left of a robust business that was once the envy of the world. Big wooden white boats maneuvered into docks all along the river, and people from every walk of life crossed the gangplanks. The passengers' experiences aboard might not have been written in the history books, but many were reported in the newspapers.

Captain Samuel Schuyler added a "cookie jar" pilothouse to his home in 1865, a style popular until about 1870. *Photo Tom Allison.*

When I bought a house across the street from a mansion once owned by one of these steamboat captains, Samuel Schuyler, I became curious about his life and the long-gone steamboat dock only a few blocks away. In the state archives, I found a scrapbook with numerous clippings about him and some photographs of his boats on glass slides. While researching them on a website of New York newspapers, I gradually acquired a list of over one hundred other steamboats that also sailed on the Hudson River in the nineteenth century.

There were always articles about the steamers when they first came on the river. When they had an accident, they made headline news again. Life aboard was not so quiet after all. Sometimes, boilers exploded, snuffing out a dozen or more lives in a second. Occasionally, one caught fire, and passengers were given their choice of death: to be burned onboard or to be drowned in the river. A clear moonless night seemed to be the best time for passenger boats to collide with one of the many sloops and schooners sharing the waterway. Aroused from sleep, a hundred or more might struggle to find their ways to safety in the dark as the boat sank.

A few steamboats were fondly remembered for unique features or lavish appointments long after they had been removed from the river. Others summoned up recollections of the frightful catastrophes that consumed them in the end.

# 1

## *SWALLOW* (1835–1845)

In 1835, the steamboat *Swallow* came on the river sporting a deck 233 feet long and 22 feet wide, an unusually long boat for its day. It was one of many steam vessels constructed in the 1830s, but the others were only 122 to 180 feet in length. On each of its paddle boxes, a silhouette of the local bird for which it was named was painted, making it distinctive. After one season, the boat was lengthened another 25 feet and a bigger cylinder installed in the engine. The extra length added buoyancy, and lifting the boat several inches more out of the water made it faster. A shallower draft allowed it to navigate the "overslaugh," a stretch that began about five miles below Albany in the driest summers. That part of the river was an ongoing problem for steamboat pilots. Deep silt covered the river bottom, leaving the water sometimes less than 4 feet deep at low tide. As boats became larger, a helper boat was stationed there to provide a tow across as needed.

The boats of the 1830s were a marked improvement on earlier ones, and *Swallow* was a good example of the new style. The boats of the 1820s had been built like common sloops with paddle wheels instead of sails. In the following decade, the hulls were designed to cut through the water with engines that were more powerful and reliable. The public aptly called them "Hudson River Fliers." The time between New York and Albany was reduced by several hours. Passengers could leave Albany or Troy at 7:00 a.m. and get to the city by 6:00 p.m. Each boat also made twelve to fifteen intermediate landings on the way. Known as day boats, they offered only a few berths in the ladies' saloon.

*Steamboat Landing (Hudson River) at Peekskill*, W.H. Bartlett, "American Scenery," London, 1838. *New York State Archives, Albany, New York.*

Passenger comfort was important, and accommodations were greatly improved. The simple canvas awnings shading the rear deck were replaced with a second deck providing more seating space. Part of the main deck became a saloon with upholstered furniture, carpets, mirrors and paintings. The effect resembled the lobby of a quality hotel rather than the waiting rooms that the passengers had just left.

When the "Fliers" first came on the river, there were spiral staircases around each of the four spars that supported the hull of the boat. They led down to the main saloon and dining room. By the 1840s, a wide staircase made a grand entrance to the deck below. During the day, light was provided by a row of skylights. In later boats with two or three tiers of staterooms, these skylights became domes of painted or stained glass.

The foredeck was devoted to fuel and freight. The boats burned wood and consumed eighteen to twenty cords for a one-way trip from Albany to New York. This was a stack of wood four feet wide, four feet high and half the length of a football field. In fifteen weeks, a boat would burn enough wood to completely cover that field. The fuel of choice was yellow pine, which was plentiful and could be burned as soon as it was cut. Because of the pitch, it burned with an intensely hot fire. When trees were sawn into planks and timbers, the bark-covered waste had no value until it found its way into steamboat boilers and became an unexpected profit for sawmills. Great piles of wood shared the foredeck with livestock in corrals, as well as barrels and boxes of freight. More fragile cargo, passengers' trunks and other baggage were stowed below the foredeck, where there were barrels of drinking water.

Skylights, such as the one on the *Falls of Clyde* from Honolulu, Hawaii, provided light to the saloons below deck. *Photo Tom Allison.*

A cabin with berths. The style and arrangement of early accommodations has been preserved on the *Falls of Clyde*. *Photo Tom Allison.*

After two seasons, *Swallow* was again enlarged and became a night boat carrying about three hundred passengers on each trip. Two rows of narrow berths were built into the sides of the main saloon and dining saloon while the ladies' saloon at the rear of the lower deck was fitted with compartments having four berths each. The night boats were advertised as having two large mirrors in the ladies' compartment. On the first boats, there was no bedding. People just climbed, fully dressed, onto sacks filled with straw or corn husks. In 1811, two steamboats, *Hope* and *Perseverance*, advertised berths with flock mattresses, blankets and bolsters. Flock was a mixture of chicken feathers and cotton and was a little more comfortable than corn husks, but not by much. Bedbugs were a given. In those days, people propped themselves against large firm cushions. In an era when respiratory problems were prevalent, many simply could not sleep flat on their backs or sides.

In the early days, passengers were not given individual tickets but were listed on a "way bill" in the daily log in the same manner as freight. A ticket cost about four dollars. People who were getting off at intermediate stops paid less. A berth or sofa, which was an additional dollar added to the fare, was a matter of choice for them. Passengers going as far as Hudson might choose to take one so they might rest comfortably until departing sometime around 3:00 a.m. The steward would write the person's name in the log next to the number of a berth. When that list was filled, sofas—created when a stack of cane-seat benches used at mealtimes was brought into the saloons late in the evening and lashed together in pairs, onto which was laid a thin mattress—were assigned. Arranged in two rows, they did not offer privacy or comfort.[1]

The alternative accommodation was "deck passage." This was the term given by the crews to the livestock corralled with the other freight on the foredeck. It became a common epithet for those sleeping in a chair at no charge. Steamboats usually had a number of rocking chairs on board, and their long curving backs made comfortable headrests. It was "first come, first serve." When the chairs were all taken, there was always a mattress on the floor.

By the mid-1830s, whale-oil lamps had replaced candles. Fifty or more sat in wall brackets, and chandeliers brightened the saloons and cabins. White walls with ornaments in bright gold made the spaces appear larger than they were. The lamps themselves were the improved Argand style. Rather than having a cotton wick, which produced a flame not much brighter than the candles they replaced, they had a woven cotton sheath that slipped over a brass tube. Air was now drawn up both sides of the flame, making it burn brighter with no flickering. The etched-glass globes cast prism effects on the walls.

Each night boat had two assistant stewards known as "lamp boys." While they had other duties, these teenage crew members could be guaranteed hours filling the dozens of lamps with whale oil, washing the burners fouled with soot, changing the wicks as needed and buffing the globes to starlike brightness. As nighttime approached, they lit them and adjusted flames to give optimum brightness without smoking. In other parts of the boat, candles in lanterns, though offering far less light, continued to be used.

Two meals were included. Dinner was served about two hours after departure, brought out on platters and large dishes to be passed down the long tables. Sliced boiled beef and pork were the usual meats with grated horseradish for seasoning. Some passengers had no manners. One might scrape half the platter onto his plate and the one next to him the rest. "Slaw," which was shredded cabbage fried in bacon fat and seasoned with vinegar, was the predominant vegetable offered, along with tureens of applesauce and shallow pans of baked beans. Thick slices of bread and plates of butter went from hand to hand at the end of the meal in addition to great wedges of cheese and tin boxes of crackers. Beer was offered and drunk by all.

Breakfast was the cold leftovers from the night before, supplemented by bowls of coarse brown bread torn up with hot milk poured over it. Stacks of griddlecakes with pieces of butter melting between them were baked directly on the iron stove tops.[2] On leaving the dining room after breakfast, passengers dropped their tips into a decorative brass vase. Five cents was considered acceptable. Gentlemen usually dropped in a dime.

At midevening, a table was set up in the dining saloon, where spirits and beer could be bought. In season, hot punches of rum well sweetened with sugar were offered. Tea was always served in the ladies' cabin at this time. Behind closed doors, the customs leveled the social classes. This was the first time in history that ordinary men and women were traveling for pleasure; once, it was only the rich who could afford such luxury.

Steamboats helped to rewrite many social conventions. At that time, etiquette dictated that women never talk to anyone to whom they had not been formally introduced, even if they met in the home of a mutual friend. Still, in this all-female environment, controversial topics were avoided and family was never discussed. Names were not exchanged. Young women called themselves "Miss" followed by the first letter of their last name while older women used "Mistress." An evening in the company of strangers could be filled with long uncomfortable silences.

Major improvements in printing at the beginning of the nineteenth century had reduced the cost of books considerably. The steamboats *Connecticut* and *Fulton* offered the first libraries in July 1821, stocked with five hundred current titles. By the 1830s, every boat carried over a thousand. Reading was a good way to pass the time.

The spiral staircase salvaged from the *Swallow*. *Photo Tom Allison.*

Multiple copies of a monthly magazine, *Godey's Lady's Book*, could be found onboard. Each month, a paperback issue came out, and a leather-bound volume of the year was released in time for Christmas. First published in 1830, it became the favorite journal of American women for the next forty-eight years.

Sarah Josepha Hale, *Godey's* editor from 1837 to 1877, created a magazine with social consciousness and how-to creativity, a combination of *O* and *Martha Stewart Living*. She introduced the public to authors Edgar Allan Poe, Washington Irving and Nathaniel Hawthorne. Their stories were serialized over several issues. Poetry, how-to projects for needlework, a garment pattern, recipes and a piece of piano music for dancing rounded out a typical month. Talking about the most recent issue or reading aloud from it became an acceptable way to pass an evening with strangers.

It was a dark and stormy night on April 7, 1845, but the *Swallow* had seen many of those in the nearly ten years as a Troy night boat. There was nothing else to suggest it was going to be different from any other trip. The river had been open for nearly two weeks, and all the pack ice had broken up and floated out to sea, which voided it causing a problem. The river was high with a swifter current because of the melting snow fed from the Adirondack Mountains into the Hudson at that time of year.

*Swallow* and *Express* left Troy on time at 6:00 p.m. after the passengers transferring from the east- and westbound trains had boarded. Troy was the northernmost terminus for the riverboats. It was also where the trains crossed the Hudson from New England over one of the longest covered bridges in the east. The railroads accounted for much of the nighttime business and were the reason for two boats. Among the passengers boarding *Swallow* that night was a Mrs. Finche who had taken the train from Bennington, Vermont. After Mrs. Finche spent the afternoon and took tea with her friends the Shiffers, Mr. Shiffer accompanied her to the boat and wished her a safe trip. The night boat from Albany, *Rochester*, left about the same hour.

*Swallow*'s first pilot was at the wheel when the boat left the dock, turning it over to the second pilot when he went for his dinner an hour later. Sometime after taking over, the second pilot moved from the east channel to the west channel of the river close to Athens. Day boats kept to the east channel so they might dock at Hudson, which was the terminal for a rail line to Stockbridge, Massachusetts, and was an important stop. The only reason for a steamboat to be in the west channel would be for passengers bound for Athens. All boats, including night boats, preferred the east channel not only because it was deeper but also because the west was encumbered with a reed-covered shoal off shore.

The first pilot returned to the wheel about eight o'clock. Shortly after, the *Swallow* hit Dooper's Island, also known as "Noah's Brig," a fifteen-foot-high rock outcropping close to the Athens shore. Rising up on the rock, the boat momentarily stood at a steep angle before it broke in two just forward of the wheelhouse. The aft portion settled in the icy water within a few minutes. There was no explosion, though the lamps in the dining saloon were overturned, setting tablecloths on fire. Someone pulled them onto the floor, where they were extinguished in the water flooding the saloon.

It is fortunate that the accident happened in midevening. Had it been after people had retired for the night, there would not have been men on deck to quickly help passengers to safety. They threw firewood through the skylights and pulled up over one hundred trapped in the saloons. With the angle of the stern, it was impossible for anyone to navigate the spiral staircases that wound around the spars.

The dozen or more who were standing under an awning over part of the foredeck not only witnessed exactly what had happened but also walked over the brig and through shallow water to shore. Because of the darkness and the storm, others did not know they were so close to safety. Some jumped

*Loss of the Steamboat Swallow* from Nathanial Currier, New York (1845), shows damage to boat and rescue attempts by Athens residents. *Library of Congress.*

in the water to be swept away in the current. Of those who died, only four were men.

In the rescue, *Rochester* took on ninety-four very cold, wet and confused passengers and *Express* another forty. It was reported that the "boom" made by the ship hitting the rock could be heard for several miles, and people thought it was an explosion. Believing a boiler blew up, Athens sextons ran to their churches and rang the bells, the accepted alarm in times of crisis. Gathering on the shore, the rescuers built bonfires to warm the incoming passengers until they could be taken to homes and hotels.

Locals climbed into rowboats at the dock and saved many who might have perished from cold or floated away in the swift current. The reports that followed in the papers said that the three boats were traveling close to one another. They had arrived near Athens in less than two hours, which was more than half an hour earlier than usual. The faster river could have been responsible for that. Based on time and the distance covered, all three boats were traveling more than fifteen miles an hour when ten to twelve was customary. If that were the case, they might have thought they were several miles farther north on the river than they actually were. The high river would also have covered the bed of reeds beside the Athens channel, adding to the confusion.

If they believed they were farther up the river, they might have engaged in a little spirited competition. From the day the first steamboat left the Troy dock, there had been a spirited rivalry between captains and pilots on both sides of the river. Albany might carry more important passengers, but Troy's boats were making more money because of the trains. The newspaper accounts offered evidence that, today, is inconclusive. Whether one accepts the statements made by the three captains and their pilots included in the New York papers saying that there was no race, there was significant loss of life. The accounts from three major New York papers were copied by the April 10, 1845 *Philadelphia Daily Courier.* It ran thirty-one inches of detailed reports and included an engraving showing the boat broken over the rock.

The catastrophe generated many letters written in haste and grief conveying information about those aboard. One was written by Mr. H.W. Shiffer in Troy to Mr. E. Goode at 67 Greenwich Street, New York. In the custom of the day, the letter was folded so that the backside became the envelope to be sealed with black wax. In the lower left hand corner is written, "In haste," boldly underlined. There is no stamp because at that time the recipient paid the postage. If delivered to the Troy dock by 6:00 p.m., it would have gone on the night boat and been in New York the next morning. Mr. Goode would have received it by noon, and the letter carrier would have collected eighteen cents from him. At that time, the cost was based on distance, but later in 1845, the U.S. Congress established a flat rate of five cents for a letter of one sheet folded to make its own envelope. The letter reads as follows:

*April 8ᵗʰ 1845*

*Mr. Goode,*

*It is with feelings of the deepest pains I enclose these lines. You have already undoubtedly heard of the horrible accident that happened to the Steamer* Swallow *on her downward trip last evening. It is currently reported that there were a number of lives lost and among the number is Mrs. Finche who was a passenger. She came from Bennington yesterday, took tea with us and I accompanied her to the boat. My information I got from an extra that was published this noon in which Mrs. Finch's name is mentioned among those that were drowned. The steamer* John Mason *left this morning for the scene of the destruction, when it returns the news will be more definite. I am afraid hearing it will prove too true of the loss of Mrs. Finch. I can of course imagine the feelings of yourself and family. It is needless to speak of the feelings of Grandmother A. Delia Love of*

The "Swallow House" has the French doors and main entrance that were salvaged from the Deck Saloon. The bay window and veranda were later additions. *Photo Tom Allison.*

*course will take the necessary steps. You had better send some friends up immediately by return boat as there is a report that the bodys* [sic] *will be brought to Albany. I trust and pray that Mrs. Finche may in some way have escaped but such is the report as I have stated here and I of course considered it a duty to write immediately.*

*Yours in haste, Albany.*
*H. W. Shiffer.*[3]

In 1846, pilot Ira Buckman from the nearby town of Valatie obtained the salvage rights for the boat. From its timbers and planks he built a Greek Revival cottage, incorporating a door and two French windows from the deck saloon. Today, the yellow-pine planking that once covered the saloon floors has been refinished to its original beauty, and one of the spiral staircases that figured in preventing those trapped below from getting on deck winds from the basement to the second floor.

# 2

# *AETNA* (1815–1824) AND *LEXINGTON* (1835–1840)

Fires and explosions were the two greatest fears for both passengers and crews aboard steamboats. The explosion aboard the *Aetna* and the fire on the *Lexington* were early catastrophes that were remembered long after they happened. In both instances, the consequent inquiries substantiated the case presented on May 18, 1832, by a U.S. Senate subcommittee on behalf of the U.S. Treasury. All too often, the decision handed down by a coroner's jury was that the fault lay with the equipment, and no blame was put on the operators. Now the testimony given clearly showed that wrongful, though not malicious, acts by the crew played significant roles. The decision made by the U.S. Congress was that while it had a role in regulating commerce, the powers of the Constitution did not extend to the vessels engaged in commerce. Congress did recommend that the secretary of the treasury appoint inspectors of boats and boilers. The wheels of justice sometimes turn slowly. The Steamboat Act of 1852, with the enforcement of laws pertaining to it, was the beginning of the U.S. Coast Guard.

When the center boiler of the *Aetna* exploded at about 7:00 p.m. on May 15, 1824, it was not the first steamboat catastrophe. That credit goes to the *Hope* in 1811. On that particular trip, there were thirty-four people onboard—nineteen passengers and fifteen officers, crew and personal servants. Twelve were either killed outright when struck by pieces of the boiler or fatally scalded when the force of the blast swept through the saloon. Only two were passengers. If the incident had happened a half hour later while the passengers were eating, the toll might have included nearly everyone aboard.

The first five steamboats on the Hudson were built with a sail to be used as a backup in case of engine failure or running out of fuel. By the 1820s, improvements to the engines made the boats less prone to breakdown. The sails were eliminated, and boats were large enough to carry fuel for the entire trip. The problems were with the boilers. Men such as James Allaire, who began his career building engines for Robert Fulton, were self-taught. They might understand the basic principles of casting, but they were working with iron, a metal that was brittle. Understanding of tolerances and metal fatigue was just beginning to develop. Copper boilers used on the first boats stood up to high pressure better, but they were very expensive to build.

Grim reports from towns on the Mississippi and Ohio Rivers were printed in eastern papers. Boilers were exploding with some regularity. Inquests found that the problem was the silt in the water. Unless routinely and thoroughly flushed out, it would cause overheating and weakening of the metal. The companies were not willing to put their boats out of service very often for that procedure.

The eastern waters did not have the silt problem, though salt water did produce some sediment, and boats were exploding, suggesting it was human error at fault. Believing the problem lay with the size of the boiler, *Aetna*'s engine designer decided to use three instead of one. There was no problem for nine years, and then, tragedy struck. The explosion was so violent that almost everything below was demolished, the deck torn to pieces and the vessel rendered a complete wreck.[4]

"Driving Deck" such as the 1812 steam engine Crofton Pumping Station in Wiltshire, England, was found with few modifications on early steamboats. *YouTube with permission from Harry Olynx.*

In his testimony at the inquest, the engineer stated that the boilers were not carrying a full head of steam at the time and were making fifteen revolutions per minute when twenty and up to twenty-five were the custom in open water. He did confirm that the boilers were being filled at the time; however, he was not asked what their initial level was at the time of filling. His answer would have proved valuable. If nearly empty, water entering the boiler would immediately turn to steam under great pressure, explaining the blast.

Steam gauges were not required until the 1850s. Before that, at the time the boiler was installed, a tube of mercury was used to determine a safe pressure level. The balance weight on the safety valve was then set for this point, and a bolt tightened it to the beam. The arrangement looked much like the scales in a doctor's office. When there was too much steam, the valve would open until the pressure dropped to the predetermined point. Reminiscing about life aboard the early boats, captains with forty years on the river said everyone on the crew could judge the boiler's pressure by the sounds that the engine made when it was running.

An engineer who spent thirty years on the boats remarked, "In most of these cases, providing the force of the explosion didn't destroy the evidence, you would likely find a couple of monkey wrenches hanging on the steam valve that didn't belong there. Either high or low pressure was safe when properly handled like this. But when the engineer, by orders or otherwise, tried to get out of the works more than they were built to stand, something was bound to happen."[5]

Two days after *Aetna*'s explosion, an editorial in the *New York Evening Post* addressed the dangers of the high-pressure engines, naming three other offending boats: *Pennsylvania, Experiment* and *Henry Eckford*. The first two suffered the same fate within a few years. The *Henry Eckford*, which was used as a towboat for its last fifteen years, exploded in 1841 while leaving the New York dock.

Eleven days after the disaster, articles indicated that the public was still rallying for something to be done. At that time, no one thought to appeal to the government to do something about the unsafe equipment. Expecting the owners would do the right thing, impassioned pleas found their way to the papers but fell on the deaf ears of steamboat owners: "The steamboat *Henry Eckford* arrived this morning with 90 passengers, high steam pressure notwithstanding. This shows that laws are necessary to restrain people from putting such a hazard in their lives. We again appeal to the corporation to interfere and interdict our waters to high pressure boats."[6]

At the inquest, Captain Elihu Bunker was called to give testimony based on his experience. Like all the captains, his schooling was on-the-job experience.

He began as a cabin boy aboard a sloop and rose to be a sloop captain and, later, a well-known steamboat captain. His steam command began in 1818 with the *Connecticut*, which ran between New York and Providence.

In 1824, Captain Bunker was given the job of superintending the construction of the *Benjamin Franklin* for a route between New York and New Haven. He was the first captain ever put in this capacity. Taking the advice of experienced river veterans became a Hudson River tradition for the next hundred years. Reporting on the progress of the construction, one New York paper wrote:

> *Captain Bunker's experience in these kind[s] of boats will enable him to make many improvements in the disposition and safe arrangement of her machinery, and in the finish of her cabins and promenade deck. It is contemplated to have the ladies' cabin on deck, and a grand saloon or dining room under a deck of nearly 100 feet in length—Capt. B is to command her in person, and from his urbanity of manners and careful attention to his business, she will no doubt prove a safe and pleasant passage boat.*[7]

He was appointed one of the government's first steamboat inspectors in 1838. His sailing experience and twenty years with steam engines made him eminently qualified. His detailed examination of the *Aetna* was the first time "forensic testimony" involving a steamboat had ever been given in a court of law. Years later, he vividly recalled his first case:

> *For myself, I have never had but one opinion as to the real cause. There were three boilers lying horizontally, parallel to each other, bedded in a brick foundation with steam pipes and feed pipes connecting them together, and the passages to the boilers in the feed pipes were very nearly closed with the sediment or collection of salt and plaster of Paris* [lime].
>
> *The center boiler was broken in two pieces nearly in the middle, one part went overboard and the other lodged on the deck near the ladies' cabin on the starboard side. I examined the passages of the feed pipes and found them nearly closed up with the substances mentioned*
>
> *This accident must have happened more for want of skill and experience than from carelessness or neglect, as it was in that day very difficult to prevent the effects of salt water from injuring steam boilers of whatever kind of metal they might be made.*
>
> *I was the first person who discovered the means of preventing the destruction of steam boilers by the deposit of the plaster of Paris and salt*

*on the flues, was by the very simple process of repeatedly changing the water through the feed pipes. Much time and money were spent in the endeavor to prevent the injury before the accident led me to the discovery of the very simple preventative.*[8]

When a low-pressure boiler exploded a few months later on the Jersey City ferry, the public was not sure who to believe. Only one passenger was killed, but the force caused the boiler to fly in the air and land bottom side up on its brick hearth. The public continued to rail on about safety:

*The destruction of lives on board the Steamboat* Aetna *has brought about much talk on "high pressure" and "low pressure" engines, but the truth is that all boilers are dangerous, although some are more so than others. The passenger walks and sits and sleeps almost in contact with a volcano that in an instant [might] blow him to atoms. The present system of fixing machinery and boilers in the center of passenger boats is unnecessary and dangerous, whether the pressure be high or low, or the boiler of iron or copper.*[9]

The following year, John Stevens and his son Robert, boat builders in Hoboken, New Jersey, designed guards for their new steamer *Trenton*. These extended the deck beyond the hull, making the paddle boxes a part of it,

A walking beam of the towboat *Syracuse*, painted by James Bard for its owner Jeremiah Austin. *Private collection, photo Tom Allison.*

and the boilers were put there. For a brief time, boats with the new design mentioned this feature with the curious phrase, "the boilers are not on board." It did not mean the boilers would not explode but that they were far less likely to cause great harm. The placement worked favorably with the new larger pistons operating under lower pressure. The walking beam became part of the machinery on most riverboats for the next century.

The next season, the *Aetna* returned to its original route sporting a new low-pressure engine with boilers on the guards. Passengers from New York traveled more easily and comfortably up the Hudson than those who were going south. While they were once satisfied with journeys taking three to four days by horsepower and wind power, they wanted to do it the same day by steam power. Boat companies took pride in getting people to their destinations as quickly as possible. Sometimes this meant transferring from the comfort of a steamer to a stagecoach rather than a longer trip by water alone. After crossing a bay, passengers would be transferred to a caravan of stagecoaches stopping at an inn or two along the way to change horses and get some cursory refreshment in a crowded taproom.

At some point, they would again board another steamboat for the last leg of the journey. This was uncomfortable and inconvenient even in the best weather. With breakdowns, bad weather or bad roads delaying them, they might make their destinations at five minutes to midnight. Six hours late, the companies had still fulfilled their obligation of same day service:

> *Philadelphia—Citizens' Steamboat line, the only line through in one day via Bordentown by the new and shortest route, 24 miles land carriage. The Citizens' Steam Boat Line starts from New York every morning, Sundays excepted, at 6 o'clock in the low pressure steamboat* Aetna, *Capt. Sutton, for Washington, New Jersey, there takes the Citizen's Post Coaches and proceeds on to Bordentown, there takes the steamboat Pennsylvania, Capt. Kellum, and arrives at Philadelphia the same afternoon. Fare $3.50.*[10]

Steamboats fell into two categories. One was the shore boats, which ran within harbors or on rivers. They were long and narrow with a deck close to the water and had a hull about four feet deep. The other was the seaworthy steamboats, built more like traditional packet boats because they went into ocean depths and dealt with the ocean swells. The earlier ones also had masts and sails as a backup in case of engine failure. On occasion, one of the seaworthy boats would sink in a storm or from an accident involving fire with the loss of all lives. While death aboard the shore boats had sometimes exceeded twenty, it was a very rare instance when the death toll was more. The four survivors of the seaworthy steamboat *Lexington* might have wondered why they were the only ones remaining that early morning in January.

Captain Cornelius Vanderbilt had made his first fortune with steam ferries around New York. His reputation for making money quickly helped him find some backers for his next enterprise. When his venture *Lexington* made its first trip, there was no more luxurious boat afloat. Providence was an important port, the ninth-largest city in the country at the time with over eight thousand residents. It was the hub for several post roads to Connecticut and more convenient for ships bringing mail and goods from Europe than Boston. It was also an important manufacturing center for the American textile industry. Samuel Slater built the first cotton mills in nearby Pawtucket in 1790.

The boat received great praise in the press following its first voyage to Providence, one headline reading, "Fastest Boat in the World." The trip took twelve hours and twenty-eight minutes, allowing eight minutes for stops, and twelve hours and five minutes for the return trip. The *Connecticut*, which had the boxy appearance of a sloop with

A candle lantern of tin plate with glass panels reproduced for me from original at Mystic Sea Port, Mystic, Connecticut. *Photo Tom Allison.*

paddle wheels, was making the trip in eighteen hours. Since the distance from Providence to New York is 220 miles, *Lexington* was averaging 20 miles an hour, a remarkable speed. The boat presented a very different profile; it was 208 feet long and 22 feet at the beam with a hold 11 feet deep. Its 24-foot wheels were designed to turn twenty-one to twenty-three revolutions per minute. Vanderbilt had secured the firm of Bishop and Simonson to design and build it. Their vessel was hailed as exhibiting "great knowledge of mechanical principles and a peculiarly bold and independent genius... the result of the immense pressure which bears upon the stem and stern while forced through the water at so rapid a rate that the deck is an arch, thus bringing the pressure against the *ends* of the timbers and planks instead against their sides."[11]

After two years, Vanderbilt changed *Lexington*'s destination to Stonington, Connecticut, where passengers transferred to a new railroad directly to Boston. A year later, after reaping fantastic profits, he sold his boat and dock and ordered the first of his steamboats for the Hudson,

Vanderbilt never intended making his money on fares. He was a venture capitalist, first to offer a service only he provided. After a reasonable time to show a good profit, he would sell the enterprise for a substantial sum. That became seed money for the next and bigger enterprise. *Lexington*'s new owners, the New Jersey Steamship Navigation Company, paid him $60,000 for one pier and boat. He later boasted it cost him less than a third of that to build. By this time, he had partnered with James Allaire, the leading engine maker in New York. Allaire began his shop by building the condenser for Robert Fulton's *North River* steamboat, also known as the *Clermont* in 1807. He continued to make engines for the North River Steamboat Company and acquired Fulton's machine shop from the inventor's estate in 1815. When Allaire was looking for capital to expand that shop and his New Jersey iron foundry near Asbury Park, Vanderbilt became a major shareholder. Thanks to that investment, *Lexington*'s boilers and engine, the most expensive part of a boat, cost him next to nothing.

A fire aboard a steamboat on a river is enough of a catastrophe. If it happens on Long Island Sound two miles from shore on a January night, no horror could be worse. On a routine night run from New York to Stonington, a member of *Lexington*'s crew saw a fire break out where one of the chimneys met the boiler. Flames spread to the freight onboard, including thirty bales of cotton destined for Rhode Island mills. To maintain the long, sleek profile of the boat, the boilers for the low-pressure engine had been placed in the hold rather than on the guards, the new style of the 1830s. The deep hold was also perfect for stowing the firewood as well. When the fire began, the proximity to the pitch-filled pine helped fuel the holocaust.

At the inquest, one of the four survivors, Captain Hillard of the steamboat *Mississippi*, offered his observations based on his own experience. Firefighting equipment was woefully inadequate. He said that water from the suction pumps playing on the timbers was not enough to dampen the blaze at all. As the inferno spread, the silhouette of *Lexington*'s captain, George Child, was seen in the wheelhouse against the blaze.

The boat was fully engulfed within fifteen minutes. The first lifeboat was lowered in front of one of the wheels while still under way and was smashed. The other three were launched but swamped when their lines fouled. When the wreck was examined it was determined that twenty-five passengers donned life preservers tied to the rails and jumped into the icy water. Others, driven from the deck by the flames, clung helplessly to the guard braces. Those still with their wits about them threw freight overboard hoping to find something that would float.

Captain Hillard and one fireman named Cox threw the bales of cotton near the people in the water. Determining the rest of the freight was likely to sink, they jumped on the last bale where they held out until the following morning. Soon after sunrise, Cox expired, leaving Captain Hillard alone until the sloop *Merchant*, bound from Southport, came along side. The first pilot and a fireman named Smith, also clinging to cotton, were pulled aboard. The other bales once had people hanging on for dear life, but by daybreak, all were gone. Hillard believed there were 150 lost, but the pilot estimated the number was closer to 180. The fire could be seen from Norwalk and Bridgeport on the Connecticut shore where boats set out to help. Once the flames died, the wreck could not be found until dawn.

Steamboat lore has maintained this disaster happened because the tiller ropes burned through, and the *Rochester*, ten years later, was the first boat to have chains instead of hemp cables for steering. Over 170 years after the catastrophe, Captain Hillard's eyewitness account tells a very different story:

> It is stated in some of the accounts, that the tiller ropes were burned. This is not correct. Captain Hillard says positively that the boat answered her help up to the time that her engine stopped, and that had she not had metal rods and chains connected with her rudder, it would long before have been useless. That she was provided with them is indisputable.
>
> Yet the company is highly censurable for encumbering her deck with so much freight and particularly with a material so inflammable as cotton.

*Awful Conflagration of the Steamboat* Lexington launched Nathaniel Currier's career with a contract for a weekly lithograph insert in the *New York Sun. Library of Congress.*

> *Doubly censurable are they as we know that not three weeks since a fire broke out on board this same boat among the goods on deck which was not extinguished without considerable loss.*[12]

This catastrophe launched the career of a New York lithographer by the name of Nathaniel Currier (1813–1888). He began his business printing cover sheets for music and doing custom work, which did not pay the bills. When a fire engulfed the Merchants' Exchange in the heart of the business district, his print showing the heroic actions of firefighters and the flames reaching into the sky quickly sold out and went into numerous reprints. A broadside with the text "Awful Conflagration of the Steam Boat Lexington in Long Island Sound Monday Eve[g], Jan[y] 13[th]" with a list of the dead went viral and began his long career capturing the spirit of America.

## 3
# EMPIRE OF TROY (1843–1853)

The *Empire of Troy* might sound more pretentious than simply the *Empire*, but the technology-proud Trojans did not want anyone to confuse this with an earlier boat of theirs named *Troy*. This city was one of America's first industrial centers. The very best, and often the first, articles of their kind to be manufactured in America came from its factories. Residents announced whenever within earshot of someone from the other side of the river, "In Albany they only make laws, in Troy we make what people want!"

*Empire of Troy*'s maiden voyage was a contest for beauty, popularity and speed. Every possible amenity one could want while traveling was offered. There were seventy plush staterooms to be booked by any of the one thousand passengers aboard. Without boilers on the guards and a walking beam engine in the middle, the unobstructed deck became a grand saloon and promenade.

The boat had the advantage of landing in Troy, where one could make all rail connections east and west. The railroad from New York ran on the east side of the river connecting with Troy in 1851. Passengers who took an Albany boat had to travel fifteen miles north on a spur and cross the river to Troy before going on to Boston and New England. Trains from the west could connect directly with a New York steamboat in Troy.

*Empire* was the first steamboat built for the Hudson to be longer than three hundred feet, and it did not resemble the Hudson River Fliers at all. This new class was given the nickname "Steam Yachts" by an adoring public. It was the first to be powered by a pair of William Lighthall's patent horizontal engines

Troy Dock, the foot of Broadway, from a stereopticon photograph. The covered railroad bridge in the background burned down in May 1862. *Rensselaer County Historical Society, Troy, New York.*

and coal-fired boilers, introduced in 1840 in the Albany boat *North America.* No longer was a great pile of slab wood filling the foredeck. Instead, the coal was loaded through a gangway hatch into bunkers. There was no walking beam rocking back and forth. Instead, the engine extended forward of the boilers. This style had been used successfully in steamboats on the western rivers, which had one paddle wheel in the rear, and was found reliable.

The new design utilized two forty-eight-inch cylinders introduced with the first low-pressure boilers, so each wheel was propelled independently. One advantage to this design was that by engaging one wheel, the boat could turn on itself in the river rather than take over a half hour to turn around.

When horizontal engines were introduced with the first steamboats in the early 1800s, they had fifteen-inch cylinders and heavy flywheels and were dependent on high-pressure boilers. Old captains interviewed in the

1880s remembered their being slow, very noisy and prone to breakdown. In contrast, *Empire of Troy* appeared to shoot through the water like an arrow.

The public wanted to know if these bigger boats and new engines were going to be faster than the ones they knew and loved. The term *race* had been attached to some contests in the past with serious repercussions. The innocuous term "time trial" removed that stigma, but it was still a race. The Troy–New York line was always contending with the Albany–New York line for first place in the hearts of the public. Throughout the 1840s, there was a flowering of new boats on both sides commanded by a cadre of captains well known in steamboat circles. Just as Captain Smith of the *Titanic* made a name for himself long before April 1912, Captains Hancox, Pratt, DeGroot, Tupper, Schuyler, St. John and others were awash with praise in any number of newspaper articles. They were the captains who commanded each of the new steamers as it came on the river and was proclaimed larger, grander and faster than the one appearing only months before.

*Empire of Troy*'s long-anticipated maiden voyage was set for May 17, 1843. Captain Tupper of Albany's *Curtis Peck*, the latest and greatest at the moment, moved its departure that day for the same time, a challenge to a race if there ever were one. Little is known about their journey up the river other than that as each made its scheduled landings, *Curtis Peck* was pulling into every dock first. At 4:30 p.m., the Albany riverfront was crowded. All the money riding on this trip was not just for tickets. The smoke from someone's stacks could be seen in the distance. Excitement grew feverish as the distant objects drew closer, and when the distinctive yellow stripes of *Curtis Peck* could be made out, a cheer went up from the Albanians. Money changed hands.[13]

*Empire* had more accidents in its one decade on the river than other steamboats had in forty years. Its first collision was with the Nineteenth Street landing on the North River. Coming in too fast and under heavy morning fog, the pilot misjudged the dock and took out over thirty feet of heavily ballasted cribwork. Had it been a stone pier, the boat would have suffered major damage, but this time, it sustained only scarred wood, nothing broken. Six years later, it had its first mid-river collision. The victim was *Noah Brown*, a schooner filled with as much lumber as it could carry. The *Noah Brown* was an unlucky boat, having been struck in 1851 by the *Rip Van Winkle*. It also collided with the *Empire* on two different occasions. The second time, it went down so fast that *Noah Brown*'s entire crew was lost. On this particular night, *Empire of Troy* and the *Rip*, as it was affectionately called, left their respective piers with capacity ridership. It

The pilothouse detail from James Bard's *Syracuse*. Carved gilded eagles in flight were traditional steamboat figureheads. *Private collection, photo Tom Allison.*

was early in the season, but when the ice left the river like a cork from a bottle, the urge to travel always began:

> *Mr. Fellows, steward of the* Rip Van Winkle *has addressed a letter to the* Tribune *dated on board the* Rip Van Winkle *May 18 in which he says, "Coming up last evening with the steamer* Empire, *we were about half a mile astern of her, when suddenly she stopped and commenced blowing off steam. We passed her thinking nothing serious had happened till her bell began to ring for assistance. When we saw that she was sinking fast, Capt. Schuyler ordered his pilot to round the boat as soon as possible. We reached the wreck just as the water put out the fires in her boilers. IT WAS QUITE DARK AT THE TIME, and the* Empire *was in the middle of the river a little below Newburgh where it is about 2 ¾ miles wide. We found she had been run afoul by the schooner* Noah Brown *which had struck her hull. She sank to her stateroom deck in about three minutes.*
>
> *The scene was terrible and heart rending. As we came alongside of the wreck there was a great rush to get on board our boat. Some jumped in the river hoping to reach us but perished. We rescued about 200 of her passengers and crew and cut holes in her deck as a means of escape for anyone trapped below. We drew one woman out from the top of the ladies' saloon who was nearly gone, she was the last taken from the wreck. We next towed her ashore on the Fishkill Flats. Many lives must have been lost, for a great number had jumped off and been carried away by the tide before we*

*could reach them. At Newburgh we left those who had friends missing. All agree that the conduct of Capt. Schuyler of the R.V.W. was generous and manly and that all that could be done he did and did it well.*[14]

Crew aboard the stricken boat said that *Noah Brown*, heading south with no lights, was tacking into the wind and was on an approach toward the path of the steamboat. At 10:00 p.m., some passengers, principally women and children, had retired for the night to the lower cabins. When *Noah Brown*'s bowsprit pierced *Empire*'s hull, it opened a gash below the waterline at the forward gangway door, which happens to be the weakest point. The saloon deck immediately began filling with water. Passengers able to get to the upper deck wore little more than their nightclothes. Only a few had presence of mind to grab their blankets. Folklore surrounding this catastrophe says that many in the ladies' cabin did not make it above before the deck was filled above a person's shoulders with the icy water. One lady reported that she threw her infant overboard before realizing what she had done and was inconsolable. The first passenger rescued from the ladies' saloon said there were several behind her, but no one could be found. It was feared they fled into the dining room where the water was over a man's head, according to a *Rip Van Winkle* crew member.

Captain Samuel Schuyler, according to those aboard the *Rip*, acted with "coolness, discretion, and great effect." With the help of the night boat from Albany, which had just left Hudson, Schuyler pushed the hulk of *Empire* to shore before leaving passengers at Newburgh. The rest went through to Albany and didn't complain even though their final destination was supposed have been Troy. They were still alive and had stories to tell their families and friends for a long time to come. The following day, a list of the 228 passengers rescued was telegraphed to newspapers across the state. Initially, there were estimates of 20 lost in the water or unidentified. There was the hope that people would come forth to claim them or report them missing. Some from the passenger list were never found.

Early the following morning, the steamboat *John Mason* took *Empire*'s captain, William W. Tupper, and crew to secure the passengers' luggage and salvage what freight they could. By 7:00 p.m., the personal effects had been transferred and seven more bodies recovered. A small steamer, *Annette*, was reported taking excursion parties out from Newburgh during the salvage operation over the next several days charging a hefty price to satisfy the curious.

Unsubstantiated accounts suggested *Rip Van Winkle* and *Empire* had been engaged in a race at the time of the incident. That fact was denied by

Captain Tupper himself. He stated that they did pass *Rip* at the beginning because the tide was giving them an advantage. No doubt the speed with which Captain Schuyler overcame them was offered as proof of a contest. In 1851, he himself had his only collision with a boat on the river, and it was with none other than *Noah Brown*. On many occasions over his sixty-six-year career, Captain Schuyler (1813–1894) was called to testify as an expert witness on the local steamboat practices. He was a highly respected captain and citizen. Like his brother Captain Thomas Schuyler, with whom he began what was to be the largest steam towboat company on the river, he was a member of the Temperance Union and a strict Methodist. If he turned his back on dancing, drinking, card playing and gambling, one would expect he turned his back on steamboat racing as well.

On May 20, an inquest into the sinking of the *Empire* was convened. Captain Tupper stated that his boat and Schuyler's *Rip Van Winkle* left their respective piers at the same hour on a night with unremarkable weather and river conditions. Levi Smith, pilot of *Empire*, deposed that he and wheelsman Wiltsie were in the pilothouse at the time of the accident. The schooner was 50 to 100 rods (about 800 to 1600 feet) off when it was first seen. *Empire* was going moderately, and the schooner coming down fast. The steamer could not go under the schooner's stern, that is to say, swerve to miss the boat. In his statement later, Captain Schuyler confirmed that the pilot's heading for the stern was the evasive action always taken in such instances. Smith stated he stopped and backed the wheels. Convinced that the schooner was going to sink them, he decided that a stationary boat would sustain fewer injuries to his passengers.

Smith said he slacked the *Empire* as soon as he saw the schooner and testified he called to put about. He added, "The schooner had time to luff and come round twice" but apparently did not hear him. Captain Robinson of the *Noah Brown* stated he heard no call, though they were only two hundred feet away, and this was confirmed by his pilot, James Drummond.

"Mr. Burden, of Troy, was picked up floating on a dry goods box, minus his hat"[15]—that image would be remembered years later by a venerable captain reminiscing about his life on the river. He recalled as a young boy doing some shad fishing when the incident occurred. Rowing out to rescue those in the water, he saved the life of the great Troy iron manufacturer Henry Burden. Later, the eyewitness account of one of Troy's leading industrialists was published in the *New York Tribune* and widely reprinted:

> *I was passing along the main deck, and being chilly, stood near the engine at the starboard side to warm myself. The engineer was in the engine room,*

and we were conversing when I heard the sound of the gong, the first stroke of which means to "stop." In an instant a double stroke which means "reverse" indicated to my ear the close proximity of danger ahead. The engineer promptly obeyed the order, but five seconds did not elapse from the command to stop until I heard the crash on the starboard bow. The steamer careened immediately to the side on which she was struck. Looking out, I saw the schooner with her stem right in the Empire. Soon after, I heard the cry that the latter was sinking. From the slow progress of her descent, I knew a considerable time must elapse before she could go down; I thought that all was right and the captain or pilot would have given necessary orders as what should be done or give passengers intimation of their danger and advice as the emergency demanded

But no such order was given, nor advice nor warning of danger nor did any officer of the Empire come upon the main deck or near the ladies' cabin where I waited in expectation of obtaining earliest information of our situation. I heard irresponsible persons who cried out frequently "There is no danger, don't be alarmed" repeating those words when the water was over the starboard side of the main deck. There was not even a light available. I endeavored to loosen the tackle of the yawl slung at the side, filled with passengers crying out in agony for someone to lower the boat, but I could not do so for want of a lantern; and it is worthy of remark that the boat continued fastened to the steamer till it was pulled down by her under water and passengers had to escape from it to the upper deck.

It was the circumstance of a large number of light boxes filled with dry goods being on deck which floated up against the saloon deck and in my estimation kept her from entirely going down…Believing from all analogy and experience she would go to the bottom in a very few seconds, I now in the last extremity waded through the water to get hold of a box and hastened with it to the after gangway on the starboard side, taking my position on the railing, holding on by the stanchion with one hand and the box with the other, where I stood till the Empire settled down from under my feet and left me floating in the river. As I could not swim, I need not say I was in extreme danger. I was half an hour in the water, and my head only over the surface and twice under when I lost my hold and my voice calling for assistance being drowned out by cries of others. There was ever probability of my being overlooked or being run down by the Rip Van Winkle had she perceived the accident a little sooner. While in this critical position, a fishing boat, having shad on board, taking passengers from the wreck fell in with me by accident and picked me up with three others, otherwise I should certainly have been lost.[16]

The remainder of Henry Burden's letter describes his belief that the captain and crew acted incompetently. He said that the captain and pilot had probably left the vessel in the very beginning because there was no accounting of them at any time, and no one appeared to be in charge of the rescue. In his opinion, the boat was not much farther than a quarter mile from Newburgh. In its precarious situation, it could have made the dock in less than fifteen minutes, even with the schooner embedded in it, and then everyone could have stepped off the boat safely.

Burden was correct. *Empire* had been given the most modern propulsion plant of its day; there were the two engines operating the wheels separately. So even if *Noah Brown* had rendered the starboard mechanism useless, the port engine could have moved the boat even if the steering were also damaged. Instead, the command had been given to blow off steam to save the engines from explosion, a judgment call making any further progress impossible. He believed with the sloop firmly embedded, everyone could have walked to safety aboard it with the minimum of direction and confusion and with the loss of not a single life.

But Henry Burden from his position on the main deck was unaware of what was happening on the deck above him. Passenger Nathaniel Paine at the inquest testified that he threw a plank from the steamboat to the deck of the *Noah Brown* and about fifty walked to safety. He also repeated his conversation with the captain, who was standing next to him. Paine did fault the pilot for not tolling the bell immediately. The *Rip Van Winkle*, which had not yet come upon them, hearing the distress call, would have sailed directly to their aid. He said he was aboard nearly three quarters of an hour, watching *Rip* stop, back around and come down the river.

When asked at the inquest about any previous accidents in his career, Levi Smith stated he was pilot when the *Empire* struck a sloop several years before and again when she struck a pier in New York. Prior to coming aboard *Empire*, he was pilot of the steamer *Albany* when it ran into a sloop. Early in his career, he was pilot of Henry Burden's boat *Helen* when he had his rudder torn off while coming into the Troy dock. Since pilots were required to be licensed, perhaps his should have been revoked years before.

Captain Tupper gave an account of his routine that night. By ten o'clock, he had retired to his cabin. Earlier in the evening when they stopped for a boat, he did not go out when he heard the bell, as that is not unusual in the lower river. Sails always took right of way, and letting them cross one's path was not just a courteous act, it was the law. In this instance, he remained in his cabin until he heard three bells and felt the concussion.

He said he returned for his lamp and made for the schooner, ordering its sails be lowered and made fast. It was blowing off, which would have added to the catastrophe since by this time his boat was leaning into it. The schooner was helping him stay upright and not tip as it filled with water. He denied the testimony that there were a great many ladies in the lower cabins, saying it was his rule to put them higher, and estimated there were less than 30 there. He said the passenger list, now unfortunately lost, filled three pages, which would have been about 250 aboard. On nights when he was taking immigrants, he routinely had had as many as 550 to 600 aboard. Anticipating any criticism that *Rip* had left too early, he said all who could be saved had been rescued by the time Captain Schuyler gave the order to resume for Albany.

*Empire*, survivor of two collisions with the *Noah Brown*, sustained a third at 3:00 a.m. on July 16, 1853. This time, everything went wrong. Under full sail, the sloop *General Livingston* cut close across *Empire*'s bow. Throwing his wheel about to give as much leeway as possible to the sail, the pilot was broadside to the sloop. Under any other circumstances, *Livingston* would have missed *Empire* by twenty yards. For a reason, not connected with the wind, it veered around. Hitting the port side, it dislodged a boiler from its foundation and reduced the guard, paddle box and wheel to kindling wood. One explanation given for the sudden turn was that the freight had not been properly stowed and securely tied down, so it shifted. Another explanation was that by the steamer's turning broadside, the sloop was caught in the wake from the paddle wheel and was out of control.

The explosion severely scalded seven who happened to be in the passages and saloon. Superheated water from the overturned boiler flooded the lower cabins. Captain Smith ordered the bell to be rung constantly. The momentum of the impact caused the steamer to career, tip and fill with water. The appropriately named sloop *First Effort* was on the scene almost immediately, along with the propeller towboat *Wyoming* to evacuate the passengers.[17]

Considering the time of the collision and nature of it, surprisingly only eight died of steam suffocation. The single drowning was a scalded chambermaid who jumped overboard. The fourteen badly scalded were taken to the home of a Mr. Van Rensselaer in New Hamburgh, where they were nursed until they could return to their homes. He refused any compensation for his attention, saying that he hoped in the future, someone might offer someone he knew the same kindness.[18]

Repeating what *Rip* had done only eight years before, *Wyoming* pushed *Empire of Troy* into six-foot shallows, where its owners, on the advice of the boat builders, declared it was a total loss. By 1853, grand as they were, these steam yachts were being replaced by gas-lit night boats with all the amenities of hotels.

## 4

# *NIAGARA* (1843–1894) AND
# *SUNNYSIDE* (1866–1875)

Captain Samuel Schuyler could not refuse the opportunity to add the once grand passenger steamboat *Niagara* to his growing fleet of towboats in 1858. Its beauty and popularity were passé, and like the other steamboats from this era, no longer servicing the premier runs. People liked to travel by boat; there was plenty of room, even in midsummer. When the river was closed was the only time to take the trains. Their thinly cushioned benches and cramped compartments could not compare to the sofas and heavily tufted chairs on a boat. There was no fresh breeze blowing in your face, and no appetizing meal offered to break up your trip. After Samuel and his brother and business partner, Captain Thomas, stripped off the passenger decks, they were left with one of the most powerful towboats on the Hudson.

In 1880, James Schuyler, named for one of the four brothers who began the towing business, accompanied his father, Samuel, on a trip down the Hudson aboard one of the towboats. One of the latest graduates from Albany Academy, the city's premier school for boys, he had begun working in the family business. Having recently joined the newly formed Albany Camera Club, he decided to document this trip by taking pictures of a number of the family's fleet. *Niagara* was among them. Pulled up to Steamboat Square, the docks just below the canal basin, it was awaiting a tow and presented a much different picture from the James Bard portrait made about 1845 for its first owner. The staterooms were gone, leaving the hog-frame structure as its most prominent feature. It still sported the double funnels from its passenger days. Three years after this picture was taken, *Niagara*, at the age of forty, received one of Samuel Schuyler's improved engines.

Samuel Schuyler was a self-educated man like many others of his era and certainly similar to other steamboat captains. He left school at the age of twelve in 1825 and was apprenticed to a sloop captain. In the 1840s, he and his brother Thomas began a towing business with four converted boats. While his brother preferred to manage the freight-forwarding end from his office, Samuel enjoyed being on the river. Based on his own study of how the engines worked, he collaborated with Skinner and Arnold, Albany boiler makers. They built an improved system that heated the steam a second time before it went into the cylinder. He had one boiler ready to be installed in *Niagara* when he acquired the engineless *Vanderbilt*. The new boilers were in his latest acquisition before the year was out, and the boat remained in daily service until the company's fleet was sold in 1892. It was bought by the Cornell Steamboat Company, though never put back in service, and two years later was towed to the breakers in Perth Amboy, New Jersey.

*Niagara* was one of several boats to be called a "Steam Yacht" by an adoring public. Thomas and William Collyer's yard was building boats with a long sleek look that was very different from those they built in the 1830s. The foot of Twelfth Street on the East River was a popular destination for Sunday walks. Watching a skeleton slowly grow a skin and rise deck by deck invited strangers to remark to one another how much had been accomplished since the week before. No sooner was one launched than another keel was laid.

In 1843, the combined Albany and Troy Line ordered *Niagara* for its day-boat service. Both the Albany line and the Troy line each ran a day boat. With the intention of squeezing out competition from any independent line, they joined forces to operate a third boat to pick up the overflow, benefitting both companies. This monopoly had the fingerprints of its principal investor, Cornelius Vanderbilt, all over it. Using the philosophy "the enemy of my enemy, is my friend," they teamed up to control the fares. They knew it was only a matter of time before a third company would make an appearance on the river and believed that if they brought on the third boat together, no company would risk bringing on a fourth because there was not enough business to sustain it.

*Niagara* was first put under the command of Captain Albert DeGroot. He was Vanderbilt's "golden child" and could do no wrong in this magnate's eyes. His parents owned a substantial farm on Staten Island near the Vanderbilts. When his mentor started his first ferry service from there to New York, DeGroot signed on as a deckhand. Changing from sail power to steam power started the young deckhand's climb up the ladder to become a captain with a noticeable streak of arrogance in his demeanor, not unlike Vanderbilt himself.

For a brief time, the steamboat *Buffalo* tried to siphon off some business, but it was too small and slow. Two years later, the combined line was trying to squeeze out a family-owned business with a fleet of three worn-out steamboats from the 1830s, which turned out to be more competition than had been anticipated.

Captain Samuel Schuyler owned a fleet that he and his brothers Thomas, William and James bought after their father, a merchant-captain with five sloops, died in 1842. They all became sloop captains. Rising through the ranks, they sailed their father's boats to the West Indies, bringing back molasses and Turk's Island salt. When the eldest Captain Schuyler died, the brothers could not wait to exchange wind power for steam power. William became the agent in New York while Thomas became the agent in Albany. James, now a wood and coal merchant, gave the family company preferential prices for steamboat fuel. There was also enough money for the brothers to acquire substantial interest in the building of a steam yacht, as the passenger boats of the 1840s were called. When the *Rip Van Winkle* arrived on the Hudson, it quickly became serious competition for the other passenger boats. Enlarged into a night boat a couple years later, Captain Samuel Schuyler sold only the number of tickets for which there were accommodations because he would not permit deck passengers. Next to his schedule printed daily in every paper was that of his rival:

*NEW YORK ALBANY & TROY STEAM BOAT LINE—Morning Line…The new and splendid fast sailing steamer TROY, Capt. A Gorham, will leave Albany for New York from the pier at Hamilton St. Mondays, Wednesdays and Fridays—leaving Troy at 6 AM and Albany at 7 AM. For passage apply to captain on board, or at the office on the pier foot of Hamilton street.*

*The new and splendid steamer NIAGARA, Capt A. Green, will leave Albany for New York from the pier at the foot of Hamilton street on Tuesdays, Thursdays and Saturdays—leaving Troy at 6 AM and Albany at 7 AM[. P]assengers apply to the captain on board or at the office on the pier at the foot of Hamilton street.*

*Evening Line for New York…From the pier foot of State Street the splendid new steam packet boat EMPIRE will leave Albany for New York on Mondays ,Wednesdays, and Fridays, leaving Troy at 5 PM, and arrive at New York in ample time to take the steam boats east and south. For passage, berths and staterooms apply at the office on the Pier foot of State Street.*[18]

The fare, fifty cents to Newburgh and $1 to the end of the line, was mostly profit. The total cost for a trip was about $250 dollars for coal, food and wages. Every dollar above that was pure profit: "On the 4[th], the new steamboat *Niagara*, Capt DeGroot, carried 1,017 passengers up the Hudson, the greater part landed at Malden and Newburgh." Even if seven hundred people got off at Malden, there was a profit of over four hundred dollars on that one trip alone. For several years, *Niagara* maintained its popularity and ridership. In the height of the season, July 1 to September 1, 1,500 passengers crowding the decks and saloons every trip was routine. A band onboard was first tried in 1821 aboard *Chancellor Livingston*, and was enthusiastically received. Thereafter, a band was onboard all the premier boats, bringing a festive atmosphere to the crowded conditions. When poor weather drove everyone under cover, however, the party mood evaporated.

When the investors made the *Niagara* a night boat, people liked the new fares, which were lower than Captain Schuyler's *Rip Van Winkle*. However, they found themselves paying more for berths and meals. Because *Niagara* had no occupancy limit, lotteries were held for the sleeping accommodations. Unlucky people found themselves "deck only," spending the night in a chair. Schuyler was not going to let these two lines drive him off the river. He had enough money coming from his towing enterprise to run the *Rip* at a loss if necessary. One night, he offered to carry passengers for free. His rule of no deck passengers meant everyone had a bed but still paid for their meals. The combined line could not compete with that.

These ruinous fare wars came to an abrupt end with the arrival of Captain Peck's *Isaac Newton*. Its size dwarfed every other steamer, and its accommodations set a new standard for night boats. Traveling on the Hudson was going to be like a night spent in a quality hotel complete with the convenience of gaslights in the cabins. *Niagara* went back on the river as a day boat for the combined line. Schuyler sold the *Rip* to concentrate on building a larger and better towing company, which included his nemesis, *Niagara*.

*The Masses in Motion—The steamboat* Isaac Newton, *Capt. Peck, left last evening with a thousand passengers. The steamboat* Niagara, *Capt. H.L. Kellogg, left this morning with between eight and nine hundred passengers.*[19]

Before Schuyler's ownership, the steamer found itself in the headlines for a number of river accidents. Under Capt. H.L. Kellogg's command, *Niagara* burst a steam chimney, killing two firemen and injuring seven passengers. This happened while the boat and the *Roger Williams* were coming up the river in tandem. Depositions from passengers were unclear whether they were racing or not. *Roger Williams* was one of the latest boats to the river and, on the day in question, was under the command of Captain Albert DeGroot, who had a couple of exploding boats on his record including *Niagara*, his first command. Feelings ran high in the courtroom. Engineer Birdsall took the stand to refute statements made in one of the papers:

> *Court Docket—We are informed that a passenger on board the* Niagara, *heard the Captain insist upon the engineer's putting on more steam when the* Roger Williams *was evidently overhauling her. The engineer replied that it was not possible with the boiler blowers as then arranged; and that by order of the Captain he changed the gearing of the blowers which doubled their velocity; and that the boiler exploded within fifteen minutes thereafter. The captain produced an affidavit stating that this was not possible because the blowers act on a crank and not a gear*
>
> *At the inquest which followed, the Captain and the Chief Engineer Hosea Birdsall were indicted on charges of endangerment to persons under their care. The jury did not find them guilty, stating that they did not maliciously cause the boiler to explode.*[20]

The combined line did not last. *Niagara* was sold in 1848 to the Housatonic Railroad for the lucrative New York to Bridgeport run, which was also short lived. But before returning to the Hudson, there was time for a double fender bender, making a memorable trip for the passengers that night: "Steamboat Ashore—The steamboat *Niagara*, bound for Bridgeport, on Sunday evening, grounded on a rock going through Hell Gate. She was soon got off the rock, but ran ashore near the gate. No injury was sustained by the passengers." [21]

Not all accounts were catastrophes. Some would bring a smile to everyone except the passengers involved: "Robbery On board the Steamboat *Niagara*.— All the silver ware was stolen from the steamboat *Niagara* on Wednesday, just before she left Albany for New York. The theft was not discovered until after the boat had gone some twelve miles on her way and spoons were wanted for supper. One of the stewards, named Jacob Brown, who fell overboard and swam ashore, is suspected to be the thief."[22]

*Jacob Tremper* rebuilt as an excursion boat. Large open saloons on two decks replaced passenger cabins. *Schuyler Collection, New York State Archives, Albany, New York.*

Sold back to the Troy line, *Niagara* became an extra boat in the high season and advertised for excursions until 1858. The classy, sleek steam yachts that once skimmed the water found themselves replaced by boats carrying twice the number the passengers at half the price. The old steamers with many years of service in them were obsolete, and they were put to new uses.

A few, such as *Jacob Tremper*, hung on through the 1890s by catering to excursion parties. Civil War veterans from the Grand Army of the Republic would hire one for the day. Covered in flags, banners and bunting and with a band, they were a colorful addition to the harbor and river. New York State had over 400,000 veterans across the state. Those living in the city, Long Island, New Jersey and southwestern Connecticut coastal towns numbered over 300,000 and were enough to fill several excursion boats every season.

One of the most popular destinations for excursions was the fishing banks off Long Island. They were fun for all ages. Whole neighborhoods from Brooklyn would arrange for a block party aboard. One trip would be all Italian, another Hasidic, another Greek or Russian or Irish. Arrangements were made through the churches, so they were much less rowdy than similar excursions by Democratic political clubs or baseball clubs.

Another option for the older boats was towing. Many a familiar friend could be seen with thirty or more barges and canal boats in its wake. Both the Champlain Canal and Erie Canal were at their heights. Timber and stone from the north with grain, agricultural products and the output from hundreds of factories needed steamers capable of handling larger tows. Once refitted, *Niagara* played in the major leagues for the Schuyler brothers.

It was as powerful as *Cayuga* and *America*, two of the three most powerful side-wheel towboats ever built, which they already owned.

Even as towboats, these steamers faced danger. Early morning fog on the river is particularly dense in the spring and late fall when cooler night air rolls down the steep sides of the highlands onto the warm river. A pilot's judgment could be regularly tested. Samuel Schuyler had devised a system of securing the barges together in a tow. The first four were tied side to side, and the rest were tied to them stem to stern, like four strings of beads. Outside barges at the end of a long tow had a tendency to swing away from the rest.

Helper boats accompanied, corralling them through the curves and the busier lower river. Owners of the canal boats received compensation for any loss incurred while on the river. Unless caught in a severe storm, which might break the lines, ordinarily only one or two were damaged at any one time: "During the fog of yesterday morning a canal boat, loaded with grain, in tow of the steamboat *Niagara*, struck the oil dock at the Athens railroad dock, and sustained considerable damage. The boat was beached just below the shipyard at Athens."[23]

Towboats would always try to make just one last trip before ice closed the river. Sometimes, the official close did not coincide with the latest weather conditions. On November 30, 1875, while heading north, *Niagara* was caught in the ice off Kinderhook with a tow that included two schooners hoping to be loaded with lumber in Watervleit and get out of the river before it closed for the season. A drop in temperature by seven degrees meant conditions would be changing by the hour. The boats' captains feared being caught in the ice, for they would be stranded until spring.

Barges being prepared for a tow. The mules that brought them down the Erie Canal are tethered on shore. *Rensselaer County Historical Society, Troy, New York.*

Sunnyside seems small in front of an unknown steamer built sometime before this pre-1875 picture was taken. *Pruyn Room Albany Public Library, Albany, New York.*

The night boat *Sunnyside* could be seen coming toward them. It picked up extra cash carrying cargo on deck and, that night, was heavily loaded, its guards low in the water. Together with the *Golden Gate*, similarly laden, they managed to break the ice-locked *Niagara* and tow as they worked through the shoals.

*Sunnyside* was a popular day boat from 1866, one of several—including *Rip Van Winkle*, *Knickerbocker*, *Shadyside* and *Washington Irving*—associated with the region's most famous author, Washington Irving. The grand saloon's centerpiece was a massive oil painting of Irving's home Sunnyside in Tarrytown. There were others throughout the boat illustrating scenes from his many works.

By 1870, *Sunnyside* was a night boat. Some boats are accident prone, and it was one of them. On a trip down in 1870, it struck an abutment of the Congress Street railroad bridge in Troy. The impact dislocated one of the boilers, and a passenger was scalded to death. Later the same year, it ran aground on Fish House Bar between Albany and Troy, leaving a sizable hole in the hull. The following August, it caught fire from spontaneous combustion in the twenty bales of cotton on the deck destined for Cohoes' mills.

On the night of the *Niagara* rescue, the extra weight on the foredeck helped the boat work like an ice breaker. But this was not the old *Norwich*, which had been built with extra thick planks to navigate when other boats could not. A few miles south of where *Sunnyside* had left *Niagara*, a crew member discovered several seams had opened up, and pumping was started.

Unidentified stateroom hall. Daylight arches through clerestory windows. Gas fixture brass is covered in starched netting to discourage flies. *New York State Archives, Albany, New York.*

Approaching the next landing, the crew reported to the captain the boat was in danger. He tried to ride up on the ice near the shore but slid back into deep water. Trying again, the bow swung upriver, and they were stranded.

It was now two o'clock in the morning, and the temperature had dropped to five degrees below zero. The first mate and sixteen passengers were lowered in the yawl, but it capsized, drowning eleven of them. The mate was eventually able to reach the shore with a line that had been tied from *Sunnyside*'s stern to the lifeboat. How he managed to do this under the circumstances is left to the imagination. Ultimately, a rope ferry between the boat and shore was established so that the remaining passengers and crew could be hauled over. *Niagara* and its tow, unaware of the night's events they left behind, continued up the river. Declared unfit for repair, *Sunnyside* was taken to the breakers at Perth Amboy, and its engine was transplanted into the next boat to come on the river, *Saratoga*.

# 5

# *KNICKERBOCKER* (1843–1865)

When Captain Isaac Newton commissioned *Knickerbocker* for the Albany–New York night route, he ordered it to be fitted with 70 staterooms having four berths and 12 elegantly furnished family staterooms each sleeping eight on the main promenade deck. The total number of staterooms was an unheard of 303. After the evening dinner had concluded, there were additional berths made up in alcoves off the dining saloon so that six hundred passengers could have a good night's sleep.

No one before had made such an effort to outfit a night boat. Newton gave the boat an aura of exclusivity when he placed advertisements in the shipping news. They looked like "calling cards." Announcing its departure schedule more than two weeks ahead of the first trip, they told the public to book their passage soon, stating, "No tickets beyond those for the berths and staterooms will be sold." He also placed an advertisement for the public to view the furnishings they would find on board:

*Exhibition of Splendid Furniture—There is a splendid collection of furniture at the establishment of Mr. William Wallace No. 170 Fulton Street. It may be seen by any who are pleased to call during this afternoon and tomorrow. It has been manufactured by Mr. Wallace for the new steamboat Knickerbocker and consists of the sofas, couches, divans, centre tables, chairs &c ordered. A look at it will highly repay the visitor.*[24]

Steamboat *Knickerbocker* at Albany. Currier and Ives lithographs are among the few available images showing how the once familiar steamers looked. *Private Collection.*

Pictures of the boat and the name *Knickerbocker* were found everywhere, including the advertising columns. The arrival of a new steamboat was heralded in places where it was least expected. To have one's latest goods delivered on the premier passenger boat suggested they were special. Only a limited amount of cargo space was available for commercial goods there. No one would think of saying that their newest merchandise came on the older boats that stopped at every landing and carried common dry goods and freight: "Just received this morning by the steamboat *Knickerbocker* from New York, a splendid assortment of Ladies' Fancy Millinery, ribbons and artificial flowers of all description—Parisian Warerooms 71 Broadway."[25]

In the contest for the popularity prize, extra points go to the boat whose name is on the lips—or, in some cases, fingers—of the most people. Copies of the music for "The Knickerbocker Schottisch" that sported an engraving of the boat on their covers appeared in the window of John Hidley's piano store in Albany's shopping district. When a customer walked in, he could hand the piece of music to a salesman who would sit down at one of Mr. Hidley's best instruments to play it for him before deciding whether to buy it. Currier and Ives also offered a lithograph of the boat drawn up to the Albany wharf. This was the first of many made after the success of the *Lexington* lithograph. The popularity of the *Knickerbocker* print proved that a steamboat didn't have to be on fire to sell prints.

*View from the Mountain House, Catskill, New York.* William Bartlett's engravings of the Hudson Valley popularized early vacation destinations. *New York State Archives, Albany, New York.*

*Knickerbocker* appealed to several different kinds of passengers who were part of what might be called "the New American Public." In the 1840s, the modern era of American commerce began. The "businessman," well dressed but not too formal, made his appearance. Men were now regularly traveling because of their work. Competition required that a representative from the company would be sent out to sell a product or promote a service. Furthermore, Albany, the state capital, was always filled with men on government business. Here was a boat designed for the man who wanted a homelike night's sleep rather than one spent like a chicken in a nesting box, which was the accommodations on the older boats.

The summer vacation, now an American institution, was also a new idea that was catching on. The Catskill Mountain House was built in 1824, and its beautiful panoramic vistas brought many seeking a diversion from the hot, crowded city streets. Saratoga Springs likewise began as a quiet resort for people coming to take hot mineral baths in a spa-like environment. Once a rail line was laid, larger hotels were built with the idea that there would be something for everyone. There were "Balls at the United States, 'Hops' at Congress Hall, Prayers at Union Hall, Juleps and Billiards for the dissipated, and Unsurpassed Mineral Water for the health-seeking."[26] The eight-bed cabins onboard were also booked by families from the city taking advantage of another new institution, the summer boardinghouse. Successful farms, both upstate and in western New England, offered accommodations by the week or season. There, city dwellers could enjoy fresh air, plenty of countryside to ramble and a sumptuous table at every meal. They were also a welcome addition to the economy of the whole town. The church might sponsor a strawberry festival or ice cream social to coax extra coins from the pockets of strangers, who were entranced by the idyllic life these country people apparently led.

The public was also becoming familiar with the sight of a woman accompanied by a porter, an assortment of cases and perhaps a trunk or two. Though customs of the day decreed that a male family member or an older woman escort her, steamboats and railroads offered a variety of services to make it easier for a woman to travel by herself. There were "Ladies Only" waiting rooms, attractively furnished with a large washroom. Female attendants assisted in any way they could. The volume of clothing that women wore and the peculiarities of how they were fastened often required help.

*Knickerbocker*'s first commander was Captain Alanson P. St. John. Tall and broad shouldered, with a Van Dyke beard, he transferred from *Rochester*. He was known for never having a steamboat collision in his career, a fact worthy of mention in his obituary. His outgoing personality and excellent service were honored by a steamboat bearing his name and commanded by the man himself. Unfortunately, it did not have as unblemished a record and was a party in one of the Hudson River's most memorable catastrophes.

*Knickerbocker*, steaming down the river on the moonless night of September 8, 1856, with 300 passengers and a deck filled with sheep and horses, collided with the wreck of a recently sunk sloop. The opposition line boat *Niagara* passed by but did not stop. The captain said in his defense that there did not appear to be an alarm, so he chose to continue. *Knickerbocker*'s captain, St. John's successor, countered that he was indicating distress and was categorically ignored. A small steamer, *Mechanic*, rescued 150 of the passengers, and local boats came out to get the rest. As the boat settled, the stock on deck in temporary corrals panicked, and all headed for the listing side. The boat turned over before sinking. Many of the sheep swam ashore; however the distress of the horses hung in the air until the last one succumbed to the water.

The boat was at first reckoned a total loss, the dislocated engine having sunk in deep mud. In a year, it was once again on the river. But by now,

Broadway from the waterfront, circa 1867. Schooners as fishing boats or loaded with freight were causes of numerous collisions. *Albany Institute of History and Art.*

another generation of steamers, larger and more elaborate, had replaced *Knickerbocker* and run away with the popularity prize. It was sold to an intermediate line out of Kingston as both a morning and evening boat to New York.[27]

Its next collision was with a sloop that happened to be afloat this time. On the clear moonless evening of March 28, 1859, sloop *Stephen Raymond*, with the maximum weight of brick and lime it could carry, crossed *Knickerbocker*'s path. It appeared that the sloop, under sail in a good wind, would easily be out of the way, so no command was made to reduce speed. As the winds are ever changeable through the Highlands, the sloop's sails dropped without warning, and because of the great cargo, it stopped. The impact of the steamboat broke the side of the sloop below the waterline, and it sank almost immediately. There was no chance for the captain (Elijah Conklin, thirty-five), mate (Peter Dalzel, twenty) and deckhand (William Hagan, eighteen) to save themselves. The boat was approaching its home dock, Hastings-on-Hudson, where three days later a very saddened town turned out for a combined funeral.

Disasters aboard steamboats on the western rivers were often included among the brief items of "Shipping News." One of the steamboat catastrophes from the Mississippi was reported in detail because of the extent of the calamity. The *Pennsylvania* exploded on June 14, 1858, with the death of more than one hundred of the three hundred aboard by scalding and flying debris. An emergency hospital was set up on the Memphis landing where those who still had a breath of life slowly rotted from the gangrene in their scalded wounds under makeshift awnings. A list of the survivors was included in the dispatch from there. Heading the list of those injured was Henry Clemens of St. Louis, the third clerk on the boat, as the *Tomkins County Democrat* reported. His brother Samuel stayed by his side, offering any comfort he could for Henry's remaining two days. Years later, Samuel recalled the experience as one of the many steamboat accidents he witnessed. He wrote, "For forty-eight hours, I labored at the bedside of my poor burned and bruised but uncomplaining brother and then the star of my home went out and left me in the gloom of despair." After Henry's death, Samuel returned to his work as a steamboat pilot. Years later, remembering his life on the Mississippi, he included the memory of his brother Henry's death in one of his books. We know Samuel Clemens more commonly as Mark Twain.

By the first days of the Civil War, *Knickerbocker* was garnering fewer passengers on its local runs. The railroad up the east side of the Hudson finally made a connection with the trains at Troy, cutting sharply into ridership between intermediate towns. People were willing to trade comfort for convenience and speed, as there were several trains a day rather than one or two boats. With a splash of fresh bunting, *Knickerbocker* became New York's first troop ship, carrying the initial 950 volunteers from the Albany Ninety-first Regiment:

> It was a pleasant and rapid trip down the noble Hudson where they landed on Governor's Island at an early hour…To remain in the vicinity of the city for a few weeks, tents were quickly set up and a small canvass village was raised…Notwithstanding the sudden change in the weather, the men all worked cheerfully to make their camp as comfortable as possible. By five o'clock, tents were pitched and many camp fires lighted around which the men gathered and warmed their somewhat numbed fingers while chatting over the events of the day…They were all uniformed before leaving Albany, and will be furnished with arms some time during the present week. [28]

Beside the account of the regiment's arrival was the report of the most recent battle: "At Munfordsville 62 rebels and 14 horses killed. Three prisoners were taken and the number of Confederate wounded and carried off unknown. The Union lost 13 killed, 13 wounded and 15 missing."[29] On March 6, 1862, *Knickerbocker* was chartered by the U.S. Quartermaster Corps to serve as a transport for the "United States Sanitary Commission." This predecessor to the Red Cross had been created in June 1861 for the purpose of providing care for the sick and wounded soldiers in the U.S. Army. Its enthusiastic director was Frederick Law Olmstead (1822–1903), who designed Central Park in New York in 1858. For three years, *Knickerbocker* served as a hospital while it collected the injured from field hospitals and brought them away from the war zone. It would return with food, clothing, medical supplies, tents, beds and other hospital furniture. Every city, town and village across the North was making a contribution to the cause if only by sending barrels of bandages. My friend Samuel Bartholomew, age ninety in 1977, recalled stories told to him by his parents and grandmother. He said his mother remembered by the end of the war that "there was not an extra sheet, shirt or pair of britches to be found in town [in Goshen, Connecticut]. Everything that could be spared went into the barrels for the boys in the entry hall of our church."

*Knickerbocker* was a steamboat designed for a millpond like the Hudson. It was not built to take the winter hurricane roaring up the eastern seaboard on February 16, 1865. It sank to its upper deck near the mouth of the Potomac. Through the closing months of the war, it became a hazard to other steamboats, like the sunken sloop that long ago sent this steamboat to the bottom of the Hudson River.

# 6
# *OREGON* (1846—1863) AND
# *C. VANDERBILT* (1847—1892)

E very captain on the Hudson had their version of what happened on the day George Law and Cornelius Vanderbilt decided, once and for all, who had the faster boat. The race was legendary, not only because the boats were considered the very best in the world but also because of the aura of power surrounding these two financial titans.

George Law (1806–1881) was one of America's early tycoons. Self-educated, he learned the trade of stonemasonry by working on the construction of the Delaware and Hudson Canals, which brought coal from Pennsylvania to the river near Kingston. He parlayed his knowledge into becoming a contractor for railroads and other canals. One was a railroad across the Isthmus of Panama, which would be the link for two steamboat lines connecting the East Coast with California. He quickly established a steamboat company that serviced both ends of the railroad. He had a monopoly on the route and was awarded the lucrative contract for carrying the United States mail to California. During the gold rush, prospectors made their way in old schooners around the tip of South America to San Francisco. There, the boats were sunk in the harbor and backfilled because the crews headed for the gold fields. Men with money, power and plans to civilize the Wild West booked passage on the steamboats of Law, Roberts, & Co.

In the midst of building these steamboats, Law ordered a luxury passenger boat for the Hudson. Launched for the 1846 season, *Oregon* cost $130,000, of which $30,000 was spent on the furnishings, an unheard-of sum. He chose Captain A.P. St. John as its commander and gave him authority

The flag from the *Oregon*. Thirty-four-star flag made by the daughters of William Clark, one of the owners, 1861–62. *Columbia County Historical Society, Kinderhook, New York. Photo by Michael Fredericks.*

over construction and furnishing the 330-foot vessel. Its seventy-two-inch cylinder engine was the world's most powerful. It was not outclassed until 1858, when the British transatlantic steamship *Great Eastern*, which laid the first transatlantic telegraph cable in 1866, was built.

Six hundred passengers could spend the night in luxury surpassing the very best hotels of the day. When St. John signed off on the designs and orders for the steamboat's outfitting, he definitely got his money's worth. Preble's *Steam Navigation*, a chronology of the firsts in the history of steamboats, included *Oregon* for its unique attention to detail. No expense was spared for luxury, comfort or innovation.

Captain St. John was a man proud of his profession and possessed a genuine respect for the traveling public. The builders claimed the *Oregon* could maintain a speed against a northwest gale and hold twenty miles an hour at sea, and, in calm waters, twenty-five. The massive brass engine in the center of the boat was treated like a work of art. Polished to a mirror shine, it reflected the floor around it, which was covered in a Brussels carpet woven in more than thirty colors, giving the effect of walking on thousands of flowers.

George Preble, who also wrote *History of the American Flag*, was the first to photograph the star-spangled banner in 1871. *Wikipedia archive.*

The center of the boat became the mid-nineteenth century equivalent of "the man cave." There were four side parlors opening onto private balconies on the guards, where one could watch the world speed past. Each was given the ambiance of an exclusive English gentlemen's club. "Power suits" and "power lunches" today are less charged with testosterone than *Oregon*'s men's saloons. Law was the first to provide extra touches for the male traveling public. He introduced a smoking room finished with Moorish designs on the walls. It was filled with tufted and fringed club chairs in brown velvet that looked like they were made from oriental rugs.

There was also a gentlemen's washroom with individual cakes of soap embossed with an image of the boat. Starched attendants helped men take off their coats. Men's shirts had collars and cuffs that were detachable. Troy had been the first to build factories employing a large, female workforce turning them out by the thousand. These pieces were removed so that passengers might freshen up in comfort, and a supply in all sizes was available to replace any that were soiled. Next to the washroom was a barber shop. Those wishing a shave were given the royal treatment by a former valet to a member of the English nobility. Law's boat claimed that the water supplied in the washroom and barber shop was from the Croton Reservoir, considered the purest water available. Law himself received a portion of his wealth from building parts of the pipe for the aqueduct that carried the water from northern Westchester County to a reservoir between Seventy-ninth and Eighty-sixth Streets in Manhattan.

The main cabin extended a full three hundred feet with more than two hundred berths. Five hundred square yards of carpeting covered the floor, and silk *satin de laine* curtains with embroidered linings hung over the berths, making the alcoves the quietest place on the boat. Irish linen sheets and bolster covers and thick Mackinaw blankets made up the beds. Top-of-the-line, thirty-pound mattresses, firm bolsters and down pillows were purchased from the leading mattress maker in New York. The name *Oregon* was worked into the designs for the Marseilles quilts on each berth. Few passengers possessed such luxury at home

A separate after cabin for the ladies featured blue and gold silk curtains. Down the center of the room was a row of white dressing tables in the French-boudoir style. Each standing mirror had two adjustable side mirrors that reflected the viewer's profile.

In the seventy-foot-long ladies' upper cabin were tiers of berths and three staterooms on each side. That washroom was even more luxurious than the men's, with floor-to-ceiling mirrors and woodwork with raised flowers and leaves on the white enamel and gilt pillars. A small army of ladies' maids in dresses of a soft neutral color, starched caps and aprons attended. A clock over the door reminding the ladies that there were gentlemen waiting for them elicited comments from the occupants.

Around 250 people could sit in the dining room at once, eating off French china with *Oregon* in gold on each piece. Heavy star-cut glass from the Boston and Sandwich glassworks reflected the coin silver made in the Prince Albert pattern that was heavy and costly.

Coin silver marked "Oregon," made by Henry Salisbury, New York, circa 1830–1838. *Columbia County Historical Society, Kinderhook, New York. Photo by Michael Fredericks.*

The stateroom hall was 220 feet long and 16 wide with sixty staterooms. One was fitted as a "bridal chamber" with a wide French bedstead and delicate flowers woven into everything.[30]

George Law's competitor in the race to amass a huge fortune was Cornelius Vanderbilt. Unlike Law, who began with nothing, Vanderbilt was a scion of one of the oldest and wealthiest Dutch families in the country. From his family's large, prosperous farm on Staten Island, he could watch the smoke from the steamboats cross the horizon. He did not see a lifetime surrounded by cabbages and hogs in his future. He began his steamboat career as a second mate aboard *Bellona*. Its owner was Thomas Gibbons, the man sued by Robert Fulton's North River monopoly for control of the New York waterways. Vanderbilt began his own steamboat empire by getting a number of backers to join him to commission a boat. Then, as the profits came in, he bought them out until he had full control. His first source of income was ferry boats between New York and Staten Island, and he grew from there.

*C. Vanderbilt* appeared on the Hudson in 1847, the most recent ordered by the magnate in his personal war with Daniel Drew and George Law. All three knew a boatload of money could be made from steamers out of New York, since much of a ticket price was profit. Drew's *Knickerbocker* was the most popular way to travel until Law unveiled his "floating palace" to mine the gold in the pockets of the traveling public.

Law was proclaiming his steamer the fastest in the country and recklessly challenged every new boat to test its mettle. Vanderbilt first offered *Traveler* for the $1,000 prize. It was half the size of *Oregon*, and he thought it was a sure bet. Law didn't object. In a twenty-mile race, they ran prow to prow, and the judges called it a draw, frustrating Vanderbilt to no end. In 1847, the one-thousand-ton *Cornelius Vanderbilt* came out of the Bishop and Simonson yards (they had built the *Lexington* for him), and he could not wait for Law to challenge him again.

The commodore, as he liked being called, discovered the paddle box was not large enough to carry the boat's full name lettered in the size he wanted, so he agreed to have it read *C. Vanderbilt*. Given high marks on the shakedown cruise, it pulled alongside *Oregon* at the New York Battery on July 1, 1847, at 11:00 a.m. The route was a run to Ossining and back.

For the first twenty miles the boats were evenly matched, and they remained in tight competition until the stake boat at Ossining was in view. Law pulled ahead and began to turn, and Vanderbilt overshot the mark where he should have begun his turn. *Oregon*'s paddle wheel was damaged. One can picture the fire in the eyes of both captains as they headed back. *Oregon*'s stokers had been piling on the coal too generously on the way up. Long blue flames trailed from its stacks, a sure sign that the boilers had been overfed.

Halfway back to the battery, *Oregon*'s bunkers were empty. Law ordered stateroom doors and furniture smashed and fed to the incandescent pyres.

This boiler in Crofton, Wiltshire, England, is comparable to those of midcentury steamboats. *YouTube with permission from Harry Olynx.*

Heavily shellacked Honduran mahogany makes a very hot fire. No doubt the safety valve on the roof of the hurricane deck was rattling like a pressure cooker. It might have even had a monkey wrench or two hanging from it to raise the pressure. In a burst of speed, *Vanderbilt* was left behind in the last quarter mile.[31]

A true speed trial, the course had been run in only three hours and fifteen minutes. The crowd on shore dispersed in search of the next "Extra Edition" to find out just what happened on the river that day. The $1,000 prize handed to George Law was turned over to his cabinet makers as partial payment to put the boat back in shape again.

One year later, Daniel Drew bought *Oregon* to run with *Isaac Newton* and *Rochester* on the "People's Line" for nonstop service between New York and Albany. *Vanderbilt* remained on the Stonington route after the race. Soon it was companion to the four-piper *Francis Skiddy* from 1855 until the government began commissioning boats at the beginning of the Civil War.

Soon after the Battle of Fort Sumter, Commodore Vanderbilt approached Secretary of War Stanton offering *C. Vanderbilt* and the rest of his boats as troop carriers. The government realized that the exposed paddle boxes on a fleet of older side-wheel steamers might as well have bulls' eyes painted on them. They would be a target for every Rebel gunboat afloat. No matter how enticing Vanderbilt was making the terms, he was turned down. However, several were leased for short-term troop transports at a price of $900 to

$2,000 a day. The commodore made sure the government paid dearly for its refusal of his initial offer.

After the Union *Monitor* and the Confederate *Merrimac* fought their first and inconclusive engagement, Secretary of War Stanton contacted the commodore to privately destroy the Confederate ship. He was expecting an astronomical price for the service. Vanderbilt told him it would cost nothing, as it was his patriotic duty. Meeting with the secretary and the president, he proposed reinforcing the prow and attaching a battering ram to *Vanderbilt*. All unnecessary superstructure was stripped and the boat fitted with cannon. Machinery that had to be exposed would be padded with five hundred bales of cotton, which was not such a smart idea, remembering what happened to another Vanderbilt steamboat. Beginning on March 23, 1862, under the commodore's personal command, it sat like a cat at a mouse hole near the mouth of Norfolk Harbor. He never had a chance to put his plan into action, as the Confederates withdrew, blowing up *Merrimac* as they left.

His steamboat went back in private service on the Troy line in the fall. Captain J.W. Hancox, who had bought out the commodore's Hudson River interests, made it a night boat, and for the next decade, it shared the docks with *Skiddy*, *Rip*, *Hero* and *Connecticut*. All were boats long past their prime. When a new company called the Citizen's Troy Line bought out Hancox's interest, *Vanderbilt* and *Connecticut* were sold to Robinson, Leonard and Betts's Troy Towing Company.

Three years later, Samuel Schuyler acquired *Connecticut*, boasting one of the most powerful engines on the river and the engineless *C. Vanderbilt* from the defunct Troy Towing Company for its scrap value. Earlier that year, the strap on its walking beam sheared, and the explosive upward thrust of the piston destroyed the cylinder and much of the engine. Schuyler's bid might have been the only one made for the twenty-eight-year-old boat. He came away from the auction with enough boats to double the size of his towboat fleet:

> *Sale of Steamer Property—The Troy Towing Company sold all their* [sic] *steamers on Friday to Schuyler and Co. of Albany. The boats are the* Alida, Ontario, Jacob Leonard, Columbia *and* Vanderbilt. *They cost $600,000, and were sold for $20,000—Schuyler and Co. now own the following Steamboats: America, Connecticut, Anna, Belle, Niagara and the five boats purchased of the Troy line, total 11 steamers. The towing business is now done by two companies, Austin's line and*

*Schuyler and Co.'s line of Albany. The steamers now belonging to Schuyler and Company cost a million dollars new and are by all odds the best and most powerful steam towboats ever seen on the Hudson.*[32]

# 7

# ISAAC NEWTON (1846–1863) AND
# NEW WORLD (1846–1864)

The *Isaac Newton* was a truly extraordinary vessel. For starters, the two boilers burned four tons of coal an hour, an astronomical amount for a steamboat. It was 338 feet long and 40 feet wide, which was not much larger than others at the time, but the paddle wheels were 39 feet in diameter, the largest ever put on a Hudson River steamboat. Each of the two shafts and cranks weighed sixteen tons. To paint the boat required twenty tons of paint. The white lead that was mixed with pure linseed oil to paint surfaces exposed to the weather was another twelve tons. Nearly 2,400 yards of carpeting covered the public rooms and cabins, which required five hundred mattresses and pillows. When it was rebuilt as a night boat, it was cut in two, and 67 feet of new boat was added. That was a record for the most any boat had ever been lengthened.

*Steamboat* Isaac Newton—*Among the numerous boats that pass up and down the North River none can compare in elegance, size and convenience to the* Isaac Newton. *A thousand passengers can be amply accommodated in this floating palace, fed at a bountiful table and enjoy every comfort desired. Capt. Peck knows how to make travelers at home on his boat. But the gentleman upon whom devolved the duty of carrying out all the minute plans, so material to the comfort of the traveler is Mr. I. Acker—No man who has once been on board the* Isaac Newton *will soon forget Mr. Acker and he who goes to Albany in his company once, will desire to go again. Our Long Island friends who at this season of the year travel north, will*

*New World*, sister ship to *Isaac Newton*. Both had intricately painted glass domes covering their stateroom halls. *Albany Institute of History and Art, Albany, New York.*

> *bear in mind that the* Isaac Newton *leaves the foot of Courtlandt St for Albany on Mondays, Wednesdays and Fridays of each week at 6 o'clock in the afternoon.*[33]

The leviathan was named for Captain Isaac Newton (1794–1858), who rose from master of a Hudson River sloop to founder of the People's Line and builder of many steamboats. His son, also named Isaac Newton, was the chief engineer on the USS *Monitor* and went on to be the first engineer for New York City. Captain Curtis Peck, the builder, was most pleased with one feature. A generating plant onboard provided the complete illumination by gaslight, including the crew quarters and boiler room. Earlier boats had introduced gaslights when they became night boats, but only in the saloons and stateroom halls.

The boat's grandest feature was an amazing stained- and painted-glass dome that spanned the entire length of the grand saloon. The galleries of staterooms around it rose to a magnificent spectacle of color. A reporter compared it to Cleopatra's barge at night. The Bridal Room carpeting was said to have come from the drawing room of King Louis Philippe of France, and over the head of the bed was an antique painted altarpiece with cupid holding two doves.[34] In 1856, in order to increase the number of staterooms to equal its companion boat, the *New World*, the dome was

*The Low Pressure Steamboat Isaac Newton Passing the Palisades on the Hudson River*, Nathaniel Currier, 1855. *Albany Institute of History and Art, Albany, New York.*

replaced with another deck. The boat was not lengthened at this time but was given extra bracing. This additional weight might have been the start of *Isaac Newton*'s problems. Reports surface in the papers about this time saying it was grounded or delayed because of low tide.

In the spring, the runoff from the melting snow from the Adirondack Mountains ran uncontrolled into the Hudson. At times, the water overflowed into the streets of towns along the river. Besides the damage done by flooding, the ice that covered the river would break into small icebergs, taking out piers and boats that had been allowed to freeze in for the winter. But a late-season hurricane could guarantee as much damage. The late August 2011 Hurricane Irene flooded out of the parking lot the museum boat *Slater* and cruise boat *Dutch Apple*. A century and a half ago, this was not an exceptional occurrence: "The River—The water is still over the pier at the quay but it has fallen several inches since Monday...The night was so dark and foggy that the Steamboat *Isaac Newton* was compelled to anchor soon after leaving New York. The Telegraph informs us that she was at Poughkeepsie at 10 ½ A.M. We go to Press therefore before her arrival...Telegraph reports informing the public is a big improvement over formerly speculating what had happened."[35]

Prior to the 1830s, there was no immigration policy. America was settled by people who came for religious reasons. Many more made the six-week voyage for the chance to own the farm on which they worked and not pay rent and a portion of their crop to a landlord. Skilled craftsmen and trades people found an open market and more demand for their goods and services here than they did at home.

The building boom and Industrialization, which has been called "the Second American Revolution," included a canal connecting the Hudson west to Lake Erie and another that ran north to Lake Champlain at Whitehall. It had furnished employment for thousands of unskilled Irish and German laborers as well as hundreds more trained in quarrying and mining. After the canals opened in 1825, the immigrant workers stayed. Immigration after that was small. Passage was expensive, and the thought of moving to a foreign country daunting. Only those who could pay the fare and had someone to meet them at the dock and help get them started resettled.

The Irish famine of the 1840s changed that, bringing the first waves of immigrants who had nothing to lose. Troubles in German principalities brought many more. They needed to be out of the cities that were crowded and offered little work for them. Most came from rural areas and knew only tenant farming. The opportunities for self-sufficiency on land in the West was appealing if they could get there easily and inexpensively. The great inland settlement was accomplished as much by steamboats and railroads as by the romanticized trains of covered wagons:

> *Hungarian Exiles—Railroad Liberality—"The seventy Hungarian exiles who came up in the steamboat* Isaac Newton *on the 1ˢᵗ inst.," says the* Albany Evening Journal, *"were, we are happy to learn, promptly passed over the railroads from Albany to Buffalo, free. In this, Messers, Corning and McIntosh who represent the U&S and S&A roads anticipated the approbation of the Western Roads. Such an act of liberality cannot but impress the strangers who seek homes in America with highly favorable views of their adopted country.*[36]

*Isaac Newton*'s career was plagued with more than its share of accidents from fire, collision and an uncooperative river. Its problems could be followed with regularity throughout its career. Twice, it came close to an unexpected end but was raised and rebuilt anew. Many of its difficulties were because it was simply much larger and faster than previous boats:

> *Court Docket—The court then took up Crockett vs. The* Isaac Newton, *which was commencing yesterday. This is a suit brought by the owners of the schooner* Hero, *to recover damages for sinking the schooner by a collision with the steamboat* Isaac Newton.
>
> *The Newton was coming into her landing on the morning of July 17, 1850; there were a good many vessels scattered along, above and below her*

*pier, and the steamer, passing between a ship and a brig found the Hero right in her course. There was not sufficient time for the schooner to get out of her way, and the steamer struck her near the bow, cutting such a hole in her that she soon after sunk.*

*Another suit was brought by the owner of the cargo of wheat and flour on board the schooner and the two causes were tried together in the court below and are being argued together on appeal.*[37]

*By Magnetic Telegraph—The steamboat* Isaac Newton, *one of the two largest and most splendid of the Hudson river boats while on her way to Albany went ashore in a thick fog on the night of the 25[th] between Caldwell's and Stony Point, the passengers and freight were taken off by the Hendrick Hudson and another boat, She subsequently sunk below her cabins. The* Newton *cost $250,000.00 and is well nigh a total wreck.*[38]

*THE STEAMBOAT* ISAAC NEWTON, *heavily loaded, is on Castleton bar. She will be lightered off, The steamboat* New World *passed Hudson on her way up at seven o'clock this morning. The steamboat E. Corning Jr. arrived at noon today. She reports heavy ice below Castleton.*[39]

On the night of December 3, 1863, the starboard boiler exploded as the *Isaac Newton* was leaving Fort Lee, Yonkers, an hour from the Cortlandt Street pier. Glowing cinders rained, burning wherever they landed. Fire broke out everywhere at once. Fortunately, it was almost the end of the season, and the passenger list was very short. The Hudson catastrophes have, for the most part, happened at either end of the season, putting the fewest number of passengers at risk. Notices in the papers said the river would close within the week. *Herald*, an older shuttle from Newburgh, and *Daniel Miller*, with three barges in tow, were coming in for the night. Both pulled alongside and took on the panic-stricken passengers. Again, it was an early evening disaster, when everyone was up, and many already on the decks. Among the seventeen injured and fourteen dead were twins James and John Hodges from Troy who were found together near the top of the grand staircase overcome by the smoke. In less than five feet, they would have been on the deck and safe. This time the boat was declared a total loss:

*The explosion was like that of a cannon and instantly the steam rushed forth: the night was cold and above decks it had but little effect. The fright occasioned, however, was terrific. About one third of the passengers were* women and children and the most indescribable terror reigned...Fortunately there were cool brave men on board who checked the frantic women and shamed the cowardly men and thus saved many [who] would have recklessly rushed to the guard and thrown themselves overboard.

In ten minutes after the explosion the entire mid ships was in flames. The passengers had fortunately all rushed aft. The flames spread savagely but before their greed was satisfied Capt. John Smith of the steamer Daniel S. Miller made fast to the starboard quarters and at once set himself to work save the passengers. He succeeded in taking all off that were aft...Some of the scalded had to be brought down to the deck on ladders. On being received on board, they were most kindly and tenderly cared for.

Soon after 8 o'clock the steamer was one entire mass of flames, the Palisades were lighted up for miles with the glare of the Demon. Boats from all directions hastened to the rescue, tugs, steamers, schooners, vessels of all descriptions hastened to lend their aid. The river in the vicinity of the steamer swarmed with them. Until 2 A.M. did the flames revel and then the vessel which had been anchored at almost the moment of the calamity was burned to the water's edge. When the "walking beam" fell—which weighed about eighteen tons—it must have crashed through the bottom and the hull sank in about fifteen feet of water. It lies now about opposite [175th] street and nothing is visible but a portion of the iron framing of one of the wheels.[40]

*Harper's Weekly* was experimenting with colored illustrations when it published an account of the burning of the *Isaac Newton*. *New York State Archives, Albany, New York.*

The sheer size of *New World* impressed everyone. Though it came out the same year as *Isaac Newton*, it seemed to be larger and grander. They were comparable in size to transatlantic steamers. Riverboats had grown so large that the piers had to be redesigned. Today, lines are long when a 747 carrying only 450 travelers lands. This one boat regularly discharged 1,000 passengers with their substantial baggage on every trip in the height of the season and never less than 600. When a grand state fair was held in Albany, 1,200 people came up from New York on each trip through the duration of the fair. Someone realized that everyone did not need to board or depart at water level, so the New York pier became a two-story affair. A favorite early evening pastime was to take a stroll before dinner and watch the night boat leave for Albany.

The name given the latest boat by its superintendent of construction, Isaac Newton, suggested exceptionalism. *New World* evoked a spirit embodied in the names of some of the first Hudson steamers: *Hope, Perseverance, Constitution, Commerce* and *Union*. The builders pushed the limits. It was nearly sixty feet wide at the guards and sat a full ten and a half feet in the water.

*New World's* first commander was the beloved Captain A.P. St. John, who was justifiably proud of this boat. Its cruising speed required a mere seventeen rotations of the wheels every minute. Employing a new invention, self-feathering paddles, the movement was virtually silent with no splashing, rumbling or vibration of any kind. They were as quiet as a rowboat's oars slipping in and out again. It's best time of six hours and twenty-one minutes was a regular occurrence. Passengers marveled how a fifteen-foot piston shaft moving so slowly up and down propelled them so quickly. Newton, knowing it would fill the coffers of the People's Line faster if it became a night boat, had *New World* rebuilt into the premier traveling experience.

There were two tiers of staterooms above the main deck with eight-foot ceilings to give passengers the feeling of being in a bedroom and not in a compartment. He offered regular beds rather than the familiar berths against the wall, but they were somewhat smaller in size. His "summer beds," what we call a twin bed today, was twenty-eight inches wide and the "matrimonial," forty-six. The rest of the furniture was similarly scaled, making the rooms appear more spacious. The convenience of gaslights in every room, hall and saloon added to the atmosphere of a residence. A great oval dome with windows of stained glass shone down through the tiers of staterooms during the day.

At night, the gas chandeliers hung with long prisms of crystal sparkled and cast exotic rainbow effects. All the crystals were cleverly glued to their hooks so that they did not move with the motion of the boat, giving the effect of a stationary room. This was probably the first time this deceit was used, and it was continued into the twentieth century on *Titanic* and other transatlantic steamers. Potted palms abounded, as did vases of flowers. There was even a fountain with a fish pond to divert and amuse. Travelers said it made more noise than the paddles. Everyone slept on thick linen sheets, pastel quilts handmade in silk, surrounded by sheer bed curtains with sprays of flowers woven in. It was an elegance only a select number of passengers had at home, but on *New World*, it was anyone's for the price.

The novel idea of an a la carte meal plan was an experiment to be copied by every other boat after that. The tradition of laying a groaning board before the passengers seated at several long tables in the dining saloon was history:

> *The New Steamer* New World—*One of the novelties of the* New World *will be the manner of serving meals, which will be of the "eating house" plan of our city dining houses, ridiculously and improperly called the "European Plan"—It will certainly be a great comfort to have the privilege of taking your meals in quiet when you want them, and to know that you only pay for what you eat, so that if you wish to drink a cup of tea only, you will not have to pay for the beefsteak, fried fish, omelets, pound cake, and brandy peaches, strawberries and cream and coffee which one hungry Hoosier chooses to devour at the same table where you sit.*[41]

On October 26, 1859, off Fort Washington at the northern tip of Manhattan, a schooner cut across *New World*'s bow. The pilot signaled for the engines to be stopped. The engineer closed the valve too quickly, and the *A*-shaped wooden gallows frame snapped five feet from the top. The eight-ton iron walking beam fell and broke. As in many catastrophes today, information leaks out in stages There is the first flush of breaking news everywhere, followed by eye witness reports. Next come the reports of the experts, and finally there are the denials that there had been anything wrong in the first place. Welcome to 1859: "Steamer *New World*—12 o'clock—noon—Captain St. John returned at 11 o'clock this morning from the sunken steamer and reports that the steamer is lying in an easy condition on the bottom, the water now up to the floor of her upper state-room—nobody killed or hurt, but some pretty badly scared…The steamer has received no material damage except the breaking through the hole in the bottom by the connecting rod. The steamer was going at her usual speed when the accident occurred, no defect or flaw can be seen where the connecting rod broke."[42]

More news trickled out during the day, and it was collected together in several reports on the same page: "The New York papers say it is estimated that at least $20,000 in freight has been destroyed, and the damage to the boat cannot fall short of $75,000. The saloons are ruined, furniture destroyed and machinery rendered completely useless…The frame which supported the walking beam was quite rotten, and the only wonder is that the accident did not occur long ago."[43]

At the time of the accident, the Albany and Canal Company towboat *Ohio* was passing without a tow and turned immediately for the steamer. Wind in its favor, the sloop *Jack Downing* sailed up to the sinking vessel, and the two boats removed the passengers who silently watched the boat bottom out with their luggage. Again it was late in the season, and the passenger list was short. Their loss was a pittance compared to the balance sheet that would be shown to Mrs. Isaac Newton, owner of most of the boat's stock: "The *New World* Accident—the loss to the proprietors of the steamer *New World* growing out of the recent sinking of that noble vessel will not be far from $100,000. There was no insurance on the property."[44]

Raised and restored to service on the night line, its days were numbered. When it left the dock in the early evening of Independence Day 1864, there was a band playing onboard, and the air was electric with talk of a swift conclusion to the war before Christmas. Reports of what exactly happened aboard are vague. Witnesses said *New World* seemed to shudder and just sink in the water. There was no concussion, explosion or anything else to alarm the passengers. Almost all were on deck and unaware that the boat was filling rapidly with water. Early reports had few details and those were vague: "The steamer *New World* is up to her guards in water. Her freight has all been brought up—Her position is bad. It is feared she is hogged."[45]

It sat in the boatyards for two years. One account said that the boat could not bear the weight of the huge engine and boiler. Another hypothesized the timbers had unforeseen rot within. Speculation about its future was the topic of conversation for the evening strollers. Then, they saw the cranes lifting the massive engine into *St. John*'s hold:

> *It is stated that the Hudson river steamer* New World *is about to be sold to the government for hospital purposes.*[46]

*The steamer* New World, *formerly of the Hudson river, is being fitted up at Alexandria as a floating hospital. It is expected to accommodate about two thousand patients.*[47]

Sixteen years was not a long life for so expensive a boat. At the end of the war, as soon as the last soldiers walked, or were carried, down the gangplanks at Fortress Monroe, it was towed to the breakers.

# 8
# *ALIDA* (1847–1883) AND
# *FRANCIS SKIDDY* (1852–1864)

*A*lida and *Francis Skiddy* were the two fastest boats of their day. The real contest between them, though, was not for speed but for beauty and comfort. Many of the stops between New York and Troy were frequented by people summering in resorts such as the Catskill Mountain House. Fresh mountain air was the "cure" most often prescribed for tuberculosis, a prevalent disease of the times. Weeks in the cool environment of higher elevations, far removed from heat, smoke and dust, brought many to this early resort. Railroads from Catskill, Hudson and other river towns reached back into rural communities, which were making money on "the vacation." Those who could leave the cities in hot weather escaped the miasma of cholera and yellow fever epidemics that came from poor sanitation and mosquitoes brought in on foreign boats. Through the summer months, the papers reported the neighborhoods with the worst outbreaks and the death toll daily.

Those people wishing to imitate the European spas had their pick. Sharon Springs, west of Albany, offered hotels where one could stay while "taking the cure," which required bathing and drinking copious amounts of the natural sulfur-, magnesium- and iron-rich chalybeate waters. North of Albany, Saratoga Springs was filled with hotels, which first catered to the health conscious, but later were the places to go for gambling and horse racing.

After their breakfasts on one of the night boats landing in Albany or Troy, guests transferred to the trains, which frequently offered special cars for guests going to particular hotels. Even after it was possible to make the

"Alida Waltz" was one of several pieces given the name of a steamboat and dedicated to its captain. *New York State Archives, Albany, New York.*

entire journey by rail, people preferred the steamboat's gentle ride, the open-promenade decks, the excellent dining and, particularly, the opportunity to choose who sat next to them.

A comic song of the 1850s portrayed a typical rail journey. Each of the eight verses made fun of a different aspect of rail travel but was close to the truth: "Stranger on the left/Closing up his peepers/Now he snores amain/Like the 'Seven Sleepers'/At his feet a volume/Gives the explanation/How that one grows stupid/All from 'Association'...Ancient maiden lady/Anxiously remarks/That there must be peril/From so many sparks/Roguish looking fellow/Turning to the stranger/Says in his opinion/She is out of danger."[48]

The train was not very appealing. The tracks were not welded together and often slightly misaligned, making one's trip a series of jolts. Ash, sparks and tiny cinders from the burning wood flew into any open window. At night, flickering oil lamps down the middle of the cars swung slowly to and fro. Once underway, the conductor disappeared, so if a lamp began to smoke, it continued to do so until the end of the journey. Occasionally, a seat companion, if he were a man from the country, would climb across and spit tobacco juice into one of several cuspidors positioned down the aisle.

Although the first passenger railway in America ran from Albany to Schenectady in 1831, it was 1847 before the state legislature granted a charter for rail service up the east side of the Hudson. The towns of Poughkeepsie and Hudson, already with east–west routes, rallied the others to pressure the legislature. Of course, strong opposition would come from the steamboat owners who carried thousands of people through the season. A fledgling industry like the railroads didn't have such deep pockets. But by September 1849, the first trains were running from Thirty-first Street, New York, to Peekskill. A celebratory dinner on October 5, 1851 marked the first train to Greenbush, the town across the river from Albany.

An express ticket delivered you to Greenbush in four hours, an hour and a half more than today. If one went on to Buffalo, the whole trip took eighteen hours, including stops. When the river was closed and ferries did not run, Albany bound travelers had to go to Troy, cross the river and double back. In 1866, a bridge was built at Greenbush, and trains could finally cross the river at Albany and come into a downtown station close to State Street, which led up to the Capitol. However, its nineteen stone piers became a new hazard for steamboats and towboats.

*Alida* was a very popular day boat. It was contracted by the railroad to provide a shuttle from Poughkeepsie to Albany and Troy until the last leg was built. It was also the steamboat of choice for official functions. The ladies' saloon on the aft deck had long mirrors in elaborate gold frames alternating with similar size paintings of local scenic points that one could not see from the windows, such as Cohoes Falls, Ausable Chasm and the Helderburg Escarpment. For worldly travelers who had seen the real thing, it was favorably compared to the Galerie des Glaces at Versailles. When former president Millard Fillmore was the candidate for the Know-Nothing Party in 1856, *Alida* was decked out with one hundred yards of bunting and two brass bands for the occasion. His trip up the river was enthusiastically followed by reporters on the boat who passed off copy at each landing to be sent by telegraph to their papers' front desks. By the time the rally ended in Albany, the presses from New York to Buffalo were extolling the success of the trip:

*Clouds which had lowered and threatened, lifted and the sun shone out brightly. A cool breeze tempered his hot rays and a delightful trip was before us…on either side people waved flags and handkerchiefs in token of recognition of the steamer that conveyed the Man of the People…at unexpected points cannon were fired…At Cozzen's dock a salute was fired*

Sailors from the Japanese Embassy's escort ship, the *Kanrin Maru*, were included among the photographs taken of this historic event. *Wikipedia Commons.*

*and the band played "Hail, Columbia." W.B. Cozzens himself stepped forward and welcomed Mr. Fillmore in the name of the Americans of Orange County with a loud cheer coming from the many aboard the Alida...*

*At Newburgh, Mr. F spoke..."I confess I am a devoted and unalterable friend of the Union...I have no hostilities to foreigners. I trust I am their friend, having witnessed their deplorable condition[s] in the old country; God forbid I should add to their sufferings by refusing them any asylum in this. I would open wide the gates and invite the oppressed of every land to partake the blessings of our land and country; I would exclude only the pauper and criminal. I would be tolerant to men of all creeds and exact from all faithful allegiance to our Republican Institutions...In my view Church and State should be separate not only in form but fact—religion and politics should not be mingled."*[49]

In 1860, the first delegation from Japan came to the United States to begin a trade and friendship program. Seven years earlier, at the request of President Millard Fillmore, Commodore Matthew Perry had sailed his naval fleet into Edo Bay to compel the Japanese to send a delegation to establish trade with this country. By the time they reached New York, they were not impressed with being treated like a circus sideshow.

The peculiarly dressed women and men were received with the curiosity people had when visiting P.T. Barnum's museum exhibitions. Their first stop was San Francisco, which had a sizable Chinese population. As the Chinese and Japanese had been enemies for centuries, that made for some tense moments, and the visit hurriedly concluded. Sailing to Panama and by rail across the isthmus, their next stop was Washington D.C., where they presented the famous cherry trees as a gift of friendship with the American people.

After Baltimore and Philadelphia, New York was the last stop. Accounts report that there was no formal escort other than the crowds that flocked to stare at them. At Perth Amboy, New Jersey, they boarded *Alida* to be formally greeted before taking an excursion around the bay complete with a "substantial collation." It was noted the princes and ambassadors were given the seclusion from scrutiny and curiosity for the first time since they had left Japan.

When it came time to reckon the cost of their visit, some irregularities were found. New York City aldermen had sold tickets at inflated prices for the Japanese ball, pocketing a hefty 33 percent commission for themselves. It seems that everyone was out to make as much as they could off of the event. The $500.00 dollar fee for a two-hour excursion on *Alida* was five times what the boat would have ordinarily charged. The $2,400.00 luncheon aboard included 300 bottles of wine at the inflated price of $2.50 a bottle, a week's wages for a New York City laborer. People along the shore must have thought the steamboat, covered in Japanese and American flags, was on fire. The city was billed for 2,100 cigars. The Grand Ball was indeed spectacular but certainly twelve thousand people did not attend, though twelve thousand tickets were sold. However, the committee was billed for the "Evening Supper" for every ticket at $3.00 a plate. With the exception of Delmonico's Restaurant, four people could sit down to a restaurant dinner, exclusive of wine, for the cost of one of those plates. Throughout the evening, 7,500 bottles of wine contributed to the festivities. The total for the three days was $105,000.00, which included the $18,000.00 for all of the Japanese delegation's expenses.[50]

There was no investigation into improprieties. William Marcy Tweed, best known as "Boss Tweed" of Tammany Hall, had only been in office two years, but a political machine in the city was firmly entrenched over decades. In light of the funds taken from the public treasury in later years, this was insignificant.

Some of the Hudson River steamboats did retire from service. *Alida* spent its last two decades out of the public spotlight. The grand saloon, dining room and stateroom hall that resembled Versailles with satinwood paneling, Honduran mahogany staircase and French Salon furniture was gone. Its once snow-white profile was now nearly bereft of paint as it labored towing long convoys of coal barges out of Rondout to New York. The Belle of the River was now a gray old lady, friends and fortune gone and working hard to earn her keep. One day, readers turned to the back page of their papers to find under "Shipping News" one last mention of the much-loved boat. Some might have been surprised it was still in service:

> End of the Steamer Alida—*The famous old steamboat* Alida *was towed to what is called the "asylum" at Port Ewen, a few days since, and is now being broken up. Years ago the* Alida *was a passenger boat and in her time "Queen of the Hudson." After many years of service she was relegated to the towing fleet, and having completed her period of usefulness, will now do service as firewood and old junk.*[51]

*Alida* had held court as the queen of the river for five years. The waltz was the newest dance sensation, and the bell-shaped dresses fashionable on the best of ladies were a kaleidoscope of color as they sailed around the dance floor. Two of the most often played pieces of music on the boats were named for the steamers that inspired them. Even if one were not dancing, the catchy melodies set even the most recalcitrant toe to tapping. Onto this scene came the *Francis Skiddy*, a sensation on its maiden voyage in June 1852. In its honor was written the "Francis Skiddy Polka," linking that steamboat to another new dance introduced from the continent. The four funnels and four boilers were an experimental design. Everything about it made every other boat, and especially the *Alida*, appear small. Despite the extra weight, it boasted the fastest time trials. The engineer once remarked that he didn't believe he had ever had need to call for all the steam that was available to him.

> *The new steamboat* Francis Skiddy *to run as a day boat between this city and Albany will be [325] feet long, with other dimensions in proportion and accommodations for 1,500 passengers. Yet her draft, we are assured, will be so light that she can at all times pass the Overslaugh without detention. She has four boilers with a seventy inch cylinder. Her cabin arrangements are upon a scale of great magnificence. Her first trip will be made on or before the 21st of this month, and the present intention is to put the fare at*

*fifty cents. The* table d'hote *will be abolished, and a bill of fare will be substituted, with terms affixed from which passengers can make their selections of edibles and at what time they please. The proprietors promise the strictest punctuality in the time of starting and that no landing named in the bills shall ever be passed. Capt. Stone, formerly of the favorite boat* Alida, *is to take command.*[52]

The boats of the 1850s were moving their large saloon to the second deck. On the night boats, it was a welcome gathering place in the cool of the evening. In the contest for most beautiful boat, *Skiddy* won hands down. Its sumptuous saloon had wide doors that rolled behind the fine paneling and were invisible. The center of the ceiling was painted to look like it was open to a sky on a midsummer day with only a few snowy clouds. The doors led onto a three-hundred-foot promenade unequal to any other. It had a colorful awning over the stern of the second deck, which had always been left uncovered on previous boats.

From this vantage, passengers might enjoy the shoreline, dotted with grand country estates, many the work of Alexander Jackson Davis (1803–1892), who introduced Gothic architecture to this country. Carefully placed to take advantage of the view, each villa featured a veranda with cast-iron tables, chairs and settees. When George Collyer was choosing the furnishings for *Francis Skiddy*, he did not realize he would create an instant sensation for something not widely available, wicker furniture. Sales people in home furnishing stores were mystified by customers asking to see this new furniture made from reeds. It was lightweight, could be woven into any fanciful design and appeared completely at home in the outdoors. These comfortable chairs could be left on a porch and not be bothered by a sudden shower, or they could be carried by one person out into the yard. The steamboats introduced the public to other new products and styles. The innerspring mattress, taken for granted today, was first used in the berths. Country folk saw gaslights and, later, electric bulbs for the first time, and the grand painted glass domes of the saloons inspired people to have windows of the same material in their homes. One supplier for a later boat displayed the furniture he was providing so that customers might be able to buy it for their own homes.

The telegraph had become an asset for travelers. People were able to book tickets ahead by wire rather than sending a letter, and confirmation was returned within a couple days. This new technology was a miracle. For thousands of years, no one knew what weather was coming toward him, but with the telegraph word could be sent.

The 1857 river opened to traffic in late February, suggesting it may have been a mild winter, though ice warnings in the river and bay were ongoing. One storm in particular was severe enough to keep New York night boats at their docks. Thanks to the telegraph, people in Albany were aware of the situation and did not need to worry that some accident had befallen them. At another time, telegraphs reported the night boats to New York—*Francis Skiddy*, *Hendrick Hudson* and *New World*—had been grounded at Castleton, the first stop below Albany, and the passengers taken by rail. Exhausted passengers did not reach New York until noon the following day.[53] Delays on the trains such as these were passed on to the nearest newspapers via the telegraph. A number of these clippings of everyday life assembled together made up a human-interest story on a slow day. In one instance, papers noted that the spikes of the southbound line on one railroad bridge were discovered to have worked themselves loose, so trains were rerouted to the north line, adding to the delay. This time the problem had been discovered before the train derailed. The public read their share of those catastrophes. When Captain Thomas Schuyler was one of the most severely injured in a train collision near Poughkeepsie, he was initially taken for dead. As the telegraph relaying the news to Albany also went to the editor's desk of the *Argus*, his name headed the list of the deceased in its next edition. Fortunately, the intimation was premature, and he lived another twelve years. Sitting down to their firesides, everyone got their two cents' worth (the price of a newspaper).

The owners rebuilt *Skiddy* for the 1855 season as a night boat. They now had a real moneymaker boasting three decks of pricey staterooms from which people walked refreshed to meet the morning trains for Saratoga Springs. The added weight of the reconstruction reduced its speed, but as a night boat the extra minutes did not make a difference. Breakfast was traditionally served as the boats were crossing the Athens overslaugh, which gave a leisurely hour and a half before docking. After one last check to be sure nothing was left in their cabins, most passengers gathered genially in the saloons or on deck to catch a glimpse of the state capitol. First-time travelers were told that the great dome they saw did not belong to the government but to the Baptist church.

The shallowness of the upper river was presenting a new problem for the *Skiddy*. The added weight set the boat two feet lower in the water, and the Troy harbor was unforgiving. The builders solved this problem as they did all others: with saws, hammers and more white oak timber. They built a second hull around the old one. The added buoyancy allowed *Skiddy* to be two feet higher in the water again, thanks to a framed, six-foot gap between

*Norwich* (1836–1923), once a Hudson River Flier, was the longest-serving steamboat on the river. *Albany Institute of History and Art, Albany, New York.*

the two hulls. This fatal redesign would bring the new queen of the river to an untimely end. Yet when the changes were made, a welcoming public cheered, their favorite was back:

> *The Courier and Enquirer has the following paragraph concerning this splendid river steamer. "The Francis Skiddy," claimed by many with much reason to be the most comfortable and luxurious as well as the fastest river boat afloat, is to leave this city hereafter for Albany every morning at seven o'clock. The old Dutchmen who lived along the Hudson not long ago, had their lives been prolonged a few years to see this feat performed, would have attributed it in a great degree to the influence of "Der Duyvel"; but that potent personage has nothing to do with it; it is accomplished simply by skill and determination. The* Francis Skiddy *is made to do such things, and those who manage her do them and, as we believe, with safety.*[54]

Among the more than one hundred major accidents on the river from 1811 to 1911 was November 21, 1861, when *Francis Skiddy* collided with the schooner *W.W. Reynolds* two miles below Poughkeepsie. Anything that could go wrong did. *Reynolds*'s crew had failed to hang out stern lights, and the moonless sky made for a very black river. Its sails hung limp, and the boat probably dropped anchor for the night. Pilot Hazzard Morey realized too late there was a boat straight ahead. He had just left the dock and resumed full speed. He turned his vessel but not in time. The schooner's bowsprit shot in through a galley window and across to the adjacent boiler. In the explosion, three of the four firemen were killed outright. Four passengers on deck just above it were scalded and underwent a painful death over the next three days.[55]

Writing about the various boats on the river, one early feature writer remarked that they must be made from cork and not oak because of the speed with which they pop back up on the river after every collision. Repaired and on the route for the 1853 season, all went well for the *Francis Skiddy* until November 5, 1864. Once more, it was a moonless night, and the pilot had resumed full throttle from Van Weis Point. The boat, a little too close to shore, ran aground. There was no explosion this time, but the four boilers shifted on the impact. The framing between its two hulls collapsed, and it settled to the shallow bottom. When it was raised a week later, the salvage master said the hull looked like a crushed egg shell. The powerful engine was removed and placed in the latest boat to come on the river, the *Dean Richmond*.[56]

# *REINDEER* (1850–1852)

An 1851 issue of *Scientific American* published an article on discoveries made since 1800. The harnessing of steam power was responsible for two. Foremost was the steamboat. In 1800, all the rivers of this country were "quiet sylvan landscapes in primeval loneliness." In 1851, no less than three thousand smoke-belching creatures of all sizes plied the waterways, reducing trips from days to hours. The link with Europe had been reduced from fifty to sixteen days. Close behind was the invention of the railroad. The top speed of the first engine, Rocket, was fifteen miles an hour along a few miles of track. Scarcely a quarter century later, England had over 5,600 miles of iron roads and the continent had 20,250. America went from the 15 miles between Albany and Schenectady in 1836 to over 1,500 in that state alone.[57]

In this same issue, the journal reported excellent time made by the steamboat *Reindeer*, introduced the previous summer. An innocent challenge was made, and no one would have ever imagined that sixteen months later, this boat would be history. "Great Speed—The steamboat *Reindeer*, Capt. DeGroot, left New York yesterday morning at ten minutes past 7 and arrived here at 3 P.M.—making the passage in seven hours and fifty minutes! The R. made all seven of her usual landings between the two cities. This is one of the quickest trips on record—but still not all the *Reindeer* can do in that line, if urged to a test of her speed."[58]

James Bishop, E.J. Jacques and F.A. Williamson, the investors, were hoping they had commissioned a moneymaker. They had chosen Thomas Collyer for the builder. He was the nearest to a "brand name" in steamboat construction—the most and the best had came out of his yard over the years. Except for details in outfitting, and accommodations, *Reindeer* was indistinguishable from many of the steam yachts built in the 1840s.

Collyer's formula was a 275-foot-long, 34-foot beam and a low-pressure engine powered by a fifty-six-inch cylinder with a 12-foot stroke. He chose to put the two boilers back to back in the middle below deck rather than on the guards, and that decision sealed *Reindeer*'s fate. By this time, the low-pressure engines had a very favorable track record. Fifteen years of excellent service with no problems might have influenced his decision. Unfortunately, to that long history was added a sad footnote.

*Reindeer* was the only Hudson River steamboat to be given the name of an animal, one not even native to the region. A leaping silhouette was painted in red on the paddle boxes, and it shared a Christmas association with two earlier carriers, *Santa Claus* and *St. Nicholas*. A polka was written in its honor and dedicated to the first captain, the mercurial Albert DeGroot. Currier and Ives provided the full-color lithograph that was overprinted for the cover.

The owners introduced the boat with some excursions on the river, inviting members of the press to join a host of distinguished guests. It was imitating the debutante balls and "coming out" parties given in the best social circles. Reporters were the prospective suitors. Each one was invited to inspect the boat and enjoy the ambiance. Their feature articles were carried under the byline "By Magnetic Telegraph" across New York State and New England. The owners wanted travelers who intended to use both rail and steamboat passage to ask for *Reindeer* by name:

"Reindeer Polka" composer William Dressler is best known for his familiar march "A Life on the Ocean Wave," which is still played by military bands. *Collection of Tom Allison.*

*The* Reindeer, *as we have stated in a former notice, was built by Thomas Collyer, her engine which is a beautiful piece of machinery was manufactured at the Morgan Iron Works, the engine room is carpeted, furnished with damask arm chairs and a splendid mirror extending its entire breadth, at first sight cheating one into a belief that there are two engines at work.*

*The arrangement of her design is sort of cross between the Mississippi and the Hudson river boat and a summer craft and an improvement on both. The promenade deck is below, the ladies saloon and dining saloon on the upper deck. The decorations are all in white and gold and in a style at once chaste and gorgeous. The ladies saloon is fitted up with the greatest elegance, and from its height above the water is exceedingly light and airy. All the minor arrangements, kitchen, pantry, toilet room, officers quarters etc. have been arranged with special regard to comfort and convenience.*[59]

One of these feature writers went beyond the usual accolades of beauty, tastefulness and convenience. His homage to the importance of the engineer was prescient, like the claim *Titanic* was unsinkable. Less than two years later, *Reindeer's* chief engineer and the captain were being brought up on manslaughter charges after a boiler explosion:

*The New Steamer* Reindeer—*Through the kindness of Captain Albert DeGroot of the new steamboat Reindeer, the writer was favored with an invitation to go on an excursion to West Point on Tuesday, and having returned with the highest impressions of the boat and courteous hospitality of her commander, I cannot refrain from offering a word or two in praise of both.*

*To travel in a steamboat is not novelty now, accustomed to it as we are, how few pause to think of the mighty efforts of mind and estimate the immense amount of accumulated experience required in production of so wondrous a mass of moving matter. Notice now that as we are rushing along, a small boat crosses our path confident in the ability of the monster to avoid a fatal collision. See the finger of the pilot pressed upon a bell and by magic the motion is checked. Still too much, another touch, the ponderous engine is at rest. A slight alteration of the wonderful steering wheel gently deflects the course to her desired point within a hair's breadth.*

*Mark the attentive engineer standing in front of the powerful engine... At will he makes an almost imperceptible adjustment and straightway the boat leaps...the bell struck, he quietly raises his hand and motion almost ceases…all this accomplished without an exhibition of muscular effort. The man wills and the machine obeys…but when straps break and bolts bend, your engineer is the man between you and your death. He must think, comprehend and act on the instant. One more revolution and the whole fabric perishes or one less and the winds and waves obtain the advantage.*

*When we go down to the sea in steamships, let us not fail to recognize the high responsibility of the man whose skill and judgment controls the mighty power which becomes the agent of horrible evil, if for once his vigilant eye sleeps or his practiced hand falters…we should endeavor to encourage him by appreciating his labors.*[60]

*Reindeer's* popularity soared when singer Jenny Lind, the "Swedish Nightingale," concluded her acclaimed American tour. The boat carried her substantial entourage from New York to Albany, where she took the train to Canada, riding in a car especially decorated for her. She was the first "star" performer to make a grand tour of the United States. The *Reindeer* safe contained over $4 million in gold from those who heard her sing. Charles Dickens had toured American cities to packed houses reading from his first five novels with great success in 1842. But Currier and Ives weren't selling thousands of prints of his likeness, and additional prints were needed as covers for the sheet music with which Lind charmed the enthusiastic audiences.

The first time *Reindeer* exploded, it was under the command of Captain Albert DeGroot. The reports do not indicate if this was a "speed trial" with *Armenia* or not, but there were speculations. The two day boats always left their piers at the same hour, and it was not unusual for them to go up the river in tandem. There were some places that were popular for speed trials, and the river near the village of Barrytown was one of them. Because the accident happened at midmorning, most people would have been on deck or in the deck saloon, and nowhere near the boilers:

*Barrytown, May 6, '51--The steamer* Reindeer *blew up (probably burst her steam chimney) opposite this place just before 10 this morning. We have not ascertained the amount of damage or loss of life or limb if any has occurred. The* Armenia *was about one hundred yards off ahead; she put about and took off the passengers. The* Evening Journal *of the same date says four were injured.*[61]

Captain DeGroot already had one exploding boiler on his record—his first commission, *Niagara*. That occurred during a speed trial with *Roger Williams*, which happened to be under the command of Cornelius Vanderbilt that day, the major shareholder of both boats. While on *Reindeer*, he was censured in the press several times with letters signed by passengers from opposing boats accusing him of putting their vessel in danger. The racing did not seem to be the problem, but they complained their captain had to take evasive action to escape dire results. Racing was all right as long as passengers were safe. Years later, passengers were going to court and successfully granted awards when these charges were brought.

Everyone was still talking about the loss of *Henry Clay* when *Reindeer* exploded again sixteen months later. This time it was not while racing but as the boat was leaving the dock. Shortly after noon, Albany residents at the waterfront heard a distant "boom" from the south. There was only one thing that made that sound, and everyone dreaded the report to follow. Even so, they were not prepared to read the grim descriptions of the catastrophe:

> *Another Steamboat Accident on the Hudson—From Twenty to Thirty Lives Lost!—Twenty-five Persons Badly Injured!!*
>
> *The public sense is again shocked by another terrible accident on the Hudson river...as* Reindeer *left Malden landing, Saugerties, the return flue of the boiler which was below deck blew out and the steam rushed into the lower cabin where a number of passengers were at dinner, killing or scalding everyone in the cabin. On entering the cabin after the steam cleared 7 persons were found dead and some 50 badly scalded.*
>
> *The scene is indescribable. Scattered about were the dying and the dead (13 passengers and 12 crew all connected with the dining room), every one lacerated and mangled. Those alive, no matter how tenuously clinging to it, were immediately removed to Livingston House and nearly every room was occupied. 25 to 30 were scalded, some not expected to see the morning.*[62]

People were just beginning to gain their composure after hearing about the explosion when they learned more tragic news:

> *Discovered about 1:30 in the following morning, the boat was enveloped in fire. The very stillness of the early morning prevented the flames which rose very high from being directed toward the buildings along the dock and from there into the town which would have proven disastrous. Built two years earlier for $100,00.00, it was carrying $55,000.00 in insurance. The plan was to tow it to New York for repairs. Only the minimal crew was on board. The lines were cut hoping that it could be scuttled and saved, but it*

Pressure-relief valve detail. James Bard's painting of the *Syracuse* was probably painted from the blueprints of the boat. *Private collection. Photo Tom Allison.*

*burnt to the waterline in two hours. People gathered quietly on the dock to watch* Reindeer *silhouetted by its own flames slowly float across the river and come to rest just as the flames died out.*[63]

At the inquest, *Reindeer* was reported one hour behind its time, according to Captain Farnham and a passenger. The captain stated he knew he was late but was carrying thirty pounds of steam though he could carry forty-five. He expressed the opinion that an unforeseen fault in the boiler was the cause. No evidence was given as to the level of the water in the boiler. Had it been low, the intense heat on the flues might have caused any water added later to turn to high-pressure steam approaching three hundred degrees. John Howlett, chief engineer, wore a veil over his face to hide his terrible burns when he arrived to give testimony before the jury.[64]

For several days, the condition of the survivors was reported. The last to die was one of the worst cases and survived into the third day:

*Joseph Ebenger, a German and a waiter on board the* Reindeer *died at the Malden House where he has laid in a low condition ever since the sad occurrence. So offensive was the smell of the decomposing flesh upon his body, previous to his death, that it could be smelled for a distance of five rods from the house, and it was most disagreeable for those attending. Lime and other disinfectants were sprinkled around the room in which he lay and about the house. He was interred in the Scott burying ground at Malden. This death is the thirty first.*[65]

The details in the coroner's report described injuries found in cases of high-pressure steam. Deaths were all caused either by scalding directly or suffocation by the very hot steam.At this time, in cases of collision or explosion, no investigation went further than the coroner's inquest and coroner's jury. The verdict handed down this time was more serious. It could leave the captain and possibly the chief engineer open to personal lawsuits for loss and injury, bringing financial ruin. The first page in a new book of tort reform was written on October 1, 1852, in a letter to the paper hoping that justice for once might be done:

*The Steamboat Calamities—Indictment The* Reindeer*—We perceive that the United States District Grand Jury have found a bill of indictment for manslaughter against the Captain and Engineer of the steamboat* Reindeer, *for the explosion of the boiler on the 4ᵗʰ of September last by which many human beings were launched into eternity and some of them only after the endurance of the most hideous torture that can be conceived. This makes some amends for the silly verdict of the Coroner Jury at Malden…In the case of the Henry Clay calamity, nothing has been done as yet though we are not without hope that the day of retribution will come at last.*[66]

The press reports were detailed, including descriptions of extreme trauma. The impact had ripped up iron sheathing encasing the boiler room, and beams and timbers were propelled like torpedoes through the kitchen, pantry and dining room. They carried everything in front of them as far as forty feet. Passengers and crew enjoying the second sitting of the noon meal had the skin and flesh ripped from their bodies. Their last breath was

250-degree steam. One fireman was reported wedged among the ruins, and his body was so badly mangled that it was only by some rags once his shirt that he could be recognized.

As the steam also shot up the smoke stack, it carried all the ash and soot from the boiler and the stack in a watery black volcano to rain down on the remains of the hurricane deck smashed by the falling chimney. Miraculously, no one there was even scratched, though they were filthy and wet. Of the three hundred passengers, some fled to the bow and stern to assess their fates. Some jumped into the river, and a few drowned.

The accident could have been the fault of the captain and chief engineer from the evidence given. Usually, thirty pounds of steam was perfectly safe. However, the captain admitted to being an hour behind and could have been making twenty-two or more revolutions per minute, the steamboat equivalent of putting the pedal to the metal. Pulling into the dock, transferring passengers and casting off would have taken a maximum of five minutes. There was an extensive shut down process when making extended stops. The customary "flying landing" employed by the boats was intended to get around many of the steps. The accepted arrival was to reduce the pressure by an extended blowing off of steam while approaching and during every landing. This was a very loud roar that often startled passengers. In the inquest, Allen W. Seaman, the pilot, described how on that day, they had blown off steam at West Point as

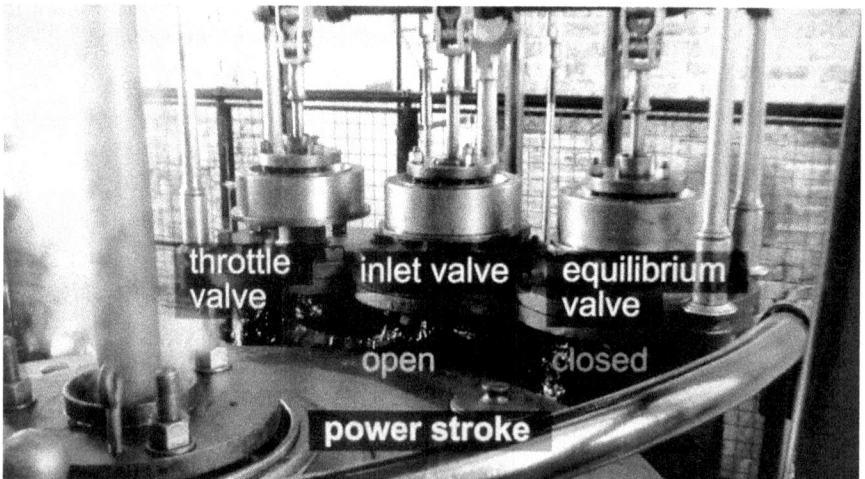

The nearest experience to an early steamboat engine room in operation is "The Fabulous 1812 Crofton Steam Engine." *YouTube with permission from Harry Olynx.*

it was a long stop, over five minutes. He said the stop at Malden was about three. On other trips they blew off steam a dozen or more times. He did note that on this occasion, the doors to the firebox were open. This would allow a draft over the fire, which could send the heat up the chimney:

> *The effect of opening the furnace doors is that they are above the fire and the cold air passing over cools the boilers and prevents the draft of the fire. If applied in time it would be sufficient to regulate and prevent much increase of steam. The practice on coming to a landing generally is to open the furnace doors from a quarter to half mile off, such has been the practice on the North river for twenty-five years past, throwing in coal at such a moment would damp the fires. It is often the case on a sudden stoppage, that it is necessary to open the safety valve. Being above the fire, this would cause a draft which would cool the fire and prevent an increase of steam. This was the action taken by the firemen of the Reindeer.*[67]

In his examination of Mr. Seaman, a fireman, the district attorney for the prosecution, Mr. Hall, read the causes of an explosion from the book *Catechism of the Steam Engine* by John Bourne. The witness said that the description "too great a pressure, insufficiency of material, flues getting read hot" was correct with his knowledge. In his summary, Mr. Hall said that appropriate measures had not been taken. "The law of Congress in 1838 required that on approaching a landing, every steamboat shall open her safety valve with a view to prevent the possibility of danger. It was not done in this case. It is said in excuse that the custom is to throw open the furnace doors instead, but the law requires the safety valve to be also."[68]

The next day, the judge delivered his charge to the jury, stating:

> *In the case of an explosion or flue collapse every person injured or lost property is to recover damages for that alone. Further it is the duty of the Captain to see that whenever a steamboat stops for whatever purpose, the safety valve shall be raised and the steam blown off. He cannot excuse himself by showing that he had another method of disposing of the steam than by raising the safety valve or showing that the state of the steam did not require it. The Captain did not follow written law and require the accepted procedure to be followed by his engineer and firemen.*[69]

The jury was sent to deliberate. After eight hours, they came back with a vote of six for and six against on a charge of manslaughter on the part of Captain Farnum: "The *Tribune* of this morning says—The trial of the Captain of the *Reindeer* amounts to nothing!"[70]

# 10
# *HENRY CLAY* (1851–1852) AND *ARMENIA* (1847–1888)

When *Henry Clay* caught fire and burned on July 28, 1852, it entered the pages of Hudson River lore as the most avoidable accident. There had been forty-three major disasters from *Paragon* in 1820 to this one, and there would be another fifty-eight in the years following until 1912. Nearly half of them were due to fire.[71] The public was regularly treated to boat collisions in their newspapers and read about at least one major catastrophe a year involving loss of a number of lives. Even jaded after forty years, readers were shocked with the details of this accident. Only eleven men drowned. Of the seventy-five identified bodies pulled from the water, forty-eight were women, twelve young children and four in their midteens. A laborer with a heavy dark beard, a boy about twenty-two and seven women were described by the coroner, but no names could be found in their belongings. The passengers had come from as far away as Ypsilanti, Michigan; Iberville Louisiana; and Boston, Massachusetts, home of one of two celebrities to die.

Onboard that day were two nationally known personalities. The tragic death of Maria Hawthorne, sister of one of the most read authors of the day, Nathaniel Hawthorne, guaranteed this accident was going to make the front page of Boston's *Herald*, *Pilot* and *Chronotype*.[72] Also to die was thirty-six-year-old Andrew Jackson Downing (1815–1852), Newburgh born and self-educated horticulturalist and architect. His book *Cottage Residences* was responsible for a new American style of architecture, and his design for the mall around the Smithsonian Institution completed in 1846 had brought him national acclaim.

As the two day boats made their way down the river, *Henry Clay* often arrived at the intermediate landings first and made extra money. Steamboat travel introduced a number of new words into the vocabulary. Passengers carrying one valise or "hand bag" could buy their tickets onboard. Those with trunks or more than one piece had to buy their tickets for a particular boat in advance, and they would be charged for "luggage." At the docks were vehicles with three or four bench seats waiting to accommodate passengers making connections by rail and were called "station wagons." The round-top trunks were designed that way for a reason. In the baggage compartment, two rows of them would be made, and the others would be turned upside down on top. This made the whole arrangement stable. They would not shift and did not need to be tied down. This system was adapted from stowing barrels in the hold. Transporting the trunks, the deckhands and dock hands would grab the strap of one trunk and the strap of another, making a line of men and luggage that snaked its way to awaiting baggage wagons or the covered porch of the ticket office.

A tag with the person's name and destination was tied on each piece before it was placed on a wagon to be brought to the boat. When the steamer pulled in, the freight was loaded through a gangway hatch at the front while passengers crossed on the aft gangway. In the baggage room, the luggage was arranged by destination. Just prior to the boat pulling in, everything to be claimed at that dock was waiting and quickly passed over to the dockhands. It was a very efficient system. It reduced many stops to only three minutes, and major stops to no more than ten.

When there were only a few passengers, the boats pulled in and used a slowly turning paddle wheel to keep the boat against the dock while passengers crossed. As the gangway was withdrawn, the wheels were reversed and the boat pulled away. Woe to the passenger who wasn't waiting for the gangway to be pushed out. Papers carried accounts of passengers falling from the gangway or the edge of the dock and sometimes drowning.

When the *Henry Clay* was built, it resembled the *Reindeer* in its construction, though it was a somewhat smaller boat. The passengers were offered a ladies' parlor on deck and a dining room below to accommodate 250 in each of two sittings at mealtime. No berths or staterooms made it light and fast. Collyer also built *Armenia* to the same formula, and they were formidable competition for steam yachts such as *Rip Van Winkle* and *C. Vanderbilt*. Originally, *Armenia* was 185 feet long and had a 28-foot beam, but in 1852, it came back from Collyer's shipyard with another 27 feet added to lift it out of the water and make it faster. During the rebuilding, Collyer improved the propulsion. The

*Armenia* is a later photograph of a Bard Painting. Flag with fifteen stars and stripes, flown 1795 to 1818, is a mystery. *New York State Archives, Albany, New York.*

paddle buckets now had a wider face, so they were moving more water with each stroke. It boasted a 50-foot-wide deck outside the guards. Once evenly matched, *Armenia* now often reached the docks ahead of the *Henry Clay*, and the rivalry might have led to the catastrophe.

*Armenia* was the only Hudson River boat to have a steam calliope, which was installed in 1858. Professor Van de Wyde transposed for its sixteen-note keyboard a repertoire of classical, religious, popular and dance music. It must have sounded weird and wonderful to people on the shore, but it made conversation aboard all but impossible. It also took a lot of steam that could have gone into the piston to power the boat. In 1864, Commodore Van Santvoort removed the instrument when he teamed *Armenia* with *Daniel Drew* and *Alida* for his new "Day Line" company. Later upgrading his fleet, he sold it to a company in Alexandria, Virginia, for excursions on the Potomac. Suffering the fate of many others, while in winter quarters, it burned to the water line on the night of January 5, 1886.[73]

On the fateful morning, *Armenia* arrived at Steamboat Square from Troy. As the "visiting boat," Albany's protocol was to let it leave the dock first. *Clay's* paddles were making their first revolutions before the other had reached the channel. They were not morning express boats, but each had sixteen landings to make. At the inquest, one angry man, the sole fare at one dock, stated that neither boat stopped, though the flag was up, indicating passengers or freight. His testimony echoed a few others that alluded that the captains were probably racing.

Bearing down on the pier at Kingston, where many passengers boarded, *Armenia* cut ahead of *Henry Clay*, which crushed some of *Armenia*'s woodwork and burst one of the steam flues. Leaving the dock, *Armenia* dropped back. The official explanation was that the engine was running on steam from only one boiler for the rest of the trip. Another offered was that the captain received threats of being thrown overboard if he continued his recklessness. The reader can decide which makes the better story.

A good distance in the lead, another two hundred boarded the *Henry Clay* at Kingston and Poughkeepsie, bringing the total to over five hundred. These were the landings that made the day's profit. In July and August, those spending time in the Berkshires were going home. They were arriving by midday trains, and an afternoon boat would carry the passengers from later trains.

Further testimony revealed that though *Armenia* was no longer racing, *Henry Clay* continued to maintain a high speed, leaving the other boat well behind. It was later discovered that Captain Tallman had lain sick in his berth since the boat left Albany, and during this time, it was under the command of Thomas Collyer, its builder. Passengers grew more alarmed as a continual shower of sparks and cinders flew from the stacks, burning through the canvas awnings to smudge and singe their clothes.

No doubt as people sat down for their noon meal below, the erratic actions of the man at the helm were the only topic of conversation. Perhaps women who carefully observed the etiquette of the day and did not talk to strangers broke the rule just this once. The meal was over and the journey to end in an hour. At 3:15 p.m., people on deck heard the dreaded cry, "Fire."

Newspaper engravings depicting catastrophes often found their way into scrapbooks, a popular pastime of the day. *New York State Archives, Albany, New York.*

A passenger going under the main shaft near the boilers said the heat was so intense that he held his handkerchief to his face as he passed. Woodwork burst into flame. In an examination of the wreck, inspectors noted that the furnace doors had not been closed and secured before turning on the blower to increase the fire's draft. The blowtorch-like flames reached the opposite wall.

Whether testimony is accurate that orders were given for passengers to go to the stern, many did. Others made for the bow. As the center of the boat went up in a great conflagration, those in the stern were left to a fiery fate they could not escape except by jumping overboard. The venerable *James Mason*, now a towboat but with nothing in tow, approached from the south. Collyer might have been the best boat builder, but he was the worst commander. Instead of taking advantage of the towboat's willingness to help, he headed for the shore over a mile away, wasting several precious minutes for the rescue. *Mason* followed in its wake, watching the flames fanning backward in a great feathery plume. Captain Harry Barber and his crew were puzzled why *Clay* was refusing their aid.

The momentum of the boat finally brought it up a gentle embankment. People in the bow dropped to safety, those in the stern nearly 140 feet away were still in deep water. The towboat pulled alongside, and rescue finally began. Those first to die were probably caught midship and jumped to their deaths. Infants were found in the arms of their mothers.[74] *Armenia* altered course to be just behind the inferno, where its crew could be seen pushing gangplanks across to the aft deck and into the water. Having stopped, the flames were no longer a threat to those passengers, who were quickly rescued.

Four men aboard a small sloop drew close, but instead of rescuing struggling victims—women weighted down with the encumbrances of their long dresses—they proceeded to coolly strip the rings and anything else they could pry from the hands of those reaching for help. Two young men in a rowboat threw a line over the sloop, climbed aboard and dispatched its despicable crew into the water with the victims. From the first alarm of fire to the last passenger pulled to safety was less than thirty minutes.[75]

Descriptions of the unidentified show the variety of people traveling that day. A twenty-two-year-old boy carried two keys, a comb, a clean shirt, a pipe, no money and a slip of paper with "James Donnahies no. 60 Laight Street New York," perhaps his destination. A woman of middle age, clean and modestly dressed, had the business card of an Albany hotel, a tin snuff box, a comb, a pocket knife and a few cents. A woman in a dress of an expensive cotton *muslin-de-laine* carried a leather pocketbook with two five-dollar bills from a Baltimore bank, nine one-dollar gold pieces, three newspaper clippings of poetry, a pair of fine black leather gloves and a diamond ring.

Another woman, about thirty, wore a string of white glass beads, an imitation diamond pin, one large crescent-shape gold earring and a pair of new leather gloves. In a small pocketbook was fifty-seven cents and what appears to be a letter of reference: "Bridget Broderick leaves with our full consent in order to be married. We have no ill will toward her whatever, sincerely wishing that in the contemplated change, she may better her condition. C.H. Palmer, W.P. Palmer 41 Irving Place July 4, 1852."[76]

Today, the cemetery near where *Henry Clay* landed contains remains of the unidentified and those identified but never claimed. One stone, a three-foot broken column symbolic of the sudden end of life, bears the names of several passengers buried in a common grave. The *New York Times* devoted over a page and a half to the catastrophe, a tribute to its tagline "All the news that's fit to print." The great statesman Henry Clay died the day after the disaster of the boat that bore his name, and papers often ran the two stories side by side.

# DANIEL DREW [1860–1865] AND DREW [1866–1902]

*D*rew and *Daniel Drew* were both named for Daniel Drew (1797–1879), one of the founders of the People's Line. Many of the riverboats were named for people who were well-regarded citizens. These two were named for a man whose business dealings left even his best friends thinking he was a double-crossing, two-faced hypocrite. His schemes to manipulate the value of railroad stock eventually cost him $1.5 million, which he could afford to lose. The millions of dollars invested by the public were never recouped. At the end of his life, with the money he acquired from ruining other men, he endowed Drew Theological Seminary, which became Drew University in Madison, New Jersey.

*Daniel Drew* dazzled the people with gas chandeliers in the style found in New York theaters and opera houses. Throughout the boat, wall brackets flickered brightly. Passengers from the city were familiar with gaslights, but people from the country were not. Unaware that the flame needed to be turned off, they simply blew it out. "Lamp Boys" regularly patrolled the passages sniffing for the telltale sulfur smell of an unlit burner. Because the gas was almost pure carbon monoxide, it was deadly in a confined space like a stateroom.

From the very beginning, steamboat fires were an imminent threat. Telegraph reports of such catastrophes, sometimes two or three a day, came to New York papers from towns along the Mississippi and Ohio Rivers. But one day, the front desks sent them the fate of two New York carriers. Riverboats had an advantage over those that crossed Long Island Sound to

*Daniel Drew* by Joseph B. Smith, circa 1860, who was a Bard contemporary known for marine scenes and townscapes. *Albany Institute of History and Art, Albany, New York.*

New England or serviced the towns along the Long Island shore. They were always close to a safe place to beach a boat in distress. The accepted course of action was to head for the nearest shore. Boats on the sound might be a long way from a coast, and the shoreline of Long Island was not always conducive to a ship making an emergency grounding. As soon as any fire was detected, passengers were ordered to the front of the boat. There, they would be safe from the flames blowing back over the deck. Such had not been the case on the *Henry Clay*, and when the middeck of any boat was fully involved, it was too late.

On the morning of March 27, 1848, *Raritan* took fire as it came up the bay. Fortunately, being near Bedloe's Island, it ran straight for shore and landed high and dry. Immediately, the engineer opened the steam valve to drop boiler pressure, averting an explosion as well. Fifty passengers disembarked onto dry land, though their possessions were lost. A ferry just leaving the dock backed up and took on three fire engines whose arrival saved most of the hull.

Two days later, *Daniel Drew* took fire as it was going down the bay with only the crew onboard. Running full steam for Governor's Island and grounding, the men safely got to shore and watched the boat burn to the water line.[77] The engine was not damaged, and the boat was rebuilt grander than before.

River traffic never ceased to expand. After the Civil War, sloops were fewer, but the long tows of canal boats and barges were new hazards. Austin, Schuyler and Cornell, the three largest companies on the river, regularly carried sixty or more canal boats behind their largest towboats. It was not

*The Grand Saloon of the Palace Steamer Daniel Drew.* Few interiors are available showing the opulence of steamboat travel. *Albany Institute of History and Art, Albany New York.*

uncommon for a half mile of tows to be found at several places along the river. On June 3, 1873, *Daniel Drew* was eighteen miles up the Hudson when it met the Austin line towboat *Ohio* with twenty-nine canal barges. As it went past, the powerful wake of the paddle wheel going at full speed broke three of them free.

The wake from a paddleboat is different from a propeller. Instead of fanning out from one point, there are two ten-foot-wide wakes close to the surface, creating an undulating effect on the river. Like beads on a string, the barges ride the wake, which is ever widening. Barges on the end of a tow swinging into this wave work themselves loose. Initially, the owner of the canal boats was awarded $233 in damages. On appeal three years later by the Austin line, the decision was reversed, maintaining a superior vessel is not necessarily liable to an inferior one in the event of injury from a swell.[78] For the rest of the century, the "Shipping News" regularly reported these collisions.

*The day line steamboat* Daniel Drew *was quite unfortunate on her trip up the river today, her rudder stock being broken as she was leaving Cornwall Landing. The boat had landed forward, and when she left the dock the wind and tide swung her stern in, and it would seem the rudder struck the dock. When she got out in the river she was beyond control,*

*Storm King Mountain* detail of J.G. Smithwick lithograph showing a typical day at one of the Hudson's bottlenecks. *Private collection.*

> *the rudder floating on its side on the water. A signal of distress given, the towboat* Anna *which was bound up with a string of boats responded coming along side and assisting the* Drew *a short distance until side wheel steamer* Ceres *and tug boat* F.A. Sears *from this city went to her aid. The* Drew *was made fast at First St, passengers and luggage were all sent ashore, people and baggage bound to points north transferred to the Hudson River railroad by way of the ferry-boat. Captain Frost and his wife and daughter who were on board the steamer, were taken riding this afternoon by Postmaster Adams. they will stay overnight at Mr. Adams' house.*[79]

*Daniel Drew*'s demise happened at the Kingston dock. As the boats did not run on Sunday, there were no passengers in danger. The crew members getting ready for the coming week were probably the only ones aboard. Midafternoon, a fire broke out in the engine house of the Delaware and Hudson Canal Company very close to the boat's mooring. A stiff breeze off the land fanned the flames toward the vessel, and in an hour, the magnificent boat with the "Grand Palace Drawing Room" was a smoldering shell. What firefighting apparatus the town possessed was intent on keeping the canal company fire from spreading. The spectacle of a double conflagration would remain with the eyewitnesses for the rest of their lives: "Sunday afternoon, the large passenger steamboat *Daniel Drew* of the Day Line caught fire at its moorings at Kingston Point and was burned to the water's edge. The loss is about $150,000. The boat was built in 1864 and was one of the largest and swiftest steamboats on the Hudson."[80]

People along the shore also remembered something else happening that day:

> *Sea Serpent in the Hudson—Rondout NY. Aug 30—Fifteen minutes before the steamboat* Daniel Drew *caught fire on Sunday afternoon the sea serpent was seen in the Hudson river between Coddington's dock and Kingston Point by a number of Rondout boatmen and boys who were swimming there. Captain R. Bush of the down-east schooner* Mary Ann *also saw it. All hands unite in saying that its head was raised about six feet out of the water and it was of the shape and general appearance of the well known anaconda or water boa of the Amazon but much larger being about two feet in diameter. The back seemed to be dark brown. From a point about six feet above the eyes, a fin appeared which extended the entire length of the body or of that portion visible, which was about fifty five feet in length. Captain Bush said the serpent lashed the water with its tail. The serpent*

Hudson Navigation Company coaling barge, 1917. Steamboats took on at least forty tons of coal for each trip. *Albany Institute of History and Art, Albany, New York.*

*was also seen by persons on the Duchess county shore. The parties say it was not sea weed they saw, and they were all "perfectly sober.*[81]

Coming on the river six years later, *Drew* was in a whole different class. Along with the *St. John*, it was one of the very best to come out of a century of steamboat building. Later boats might have been larger and carried more people, but they lacked that grand style. In one of its most popular prints, Currier and Ives celebrated the boat's last major facelift, epitomizing the skill of the builders and the expectations of the traveling public.

*St. John*'s saloon had a gallery of arched windows looking out on the scenery and, like the *Alida*, large mirrors and scenic oil paintings were installed between them. Its promenade decks had the "gingerbread" look popularized by the newly invented power scroll saw and found on everyone's verandahs. It gave the boat the appearance of a corner in the New Orleans French Quarter. *Drew*'s owners preferred a series of large staterooms on the main deck to a grand promenade. But the passengers did not miss it because they could enjoy a Fifth Avenue look at the world. The bow was enclosed with plate-glass windows, which were then making their first appearances on the fronts of the most fashionable stores. Regardless of the temperature or chance of precipitation, the Hudson passed by like one of the moving panorama shows traveling around the country. Over the years, *Drew* was modernized, and it was one of the first boats to have electric lights installed under Thomas Edison's supervision. It enjoyed a thirty-five-year run on the river, and though it had its share of running aground and collisions with tugboats in New York harbor, it was one of the few to be quietly retired:

> *Passing on the Steamer* Drew—*The steamboat* Drew, *of the People's Line which was recently bought by J.H. Gregory, of Perth Amboy, N.J., has arrived at that city and will be dismantled and converted into a barge. The* Drew *was one of the handsomest steamboats ever built. The stairways are of San Domingo mahogany and according to the president of the People's Line cost more than $60,000. Before selling it to Gregory, the owners of the boat took down the smokestack and removed a quantity of the machinery, a complete electric plant, and much else that is valuable.*[82]

# ST. JOHN (1863–1885)

*St. John* was named for Captain Alanson P. St. John, who was respected for his many years of experience. He had been the first choice to command many new steamboats that came on the river, beginning with the *Rochester* and *Knickerbocker*. When *St. John* was entered into the registry, there was no larger vessel afloat at that time except the latest British transatlantic steamer. *Great Eastern* was 692 feet long and capable of sailing around the tip of Africa from England to Australia and back, carrying enough coal for the entire trip. But passengers aboard it would never experience the attention to detail and comfort found on the Hudson River.

*St John*'s main deck was a 420-foot walk for the passengers, and the distance across the beam was the length of two New York house lots. On its first trip up the river, its passengers were treated to the sight of the U.S. Army Corps of Engineers dredging the river at the overslaugh so military boats, with a much deeper draft, could reach the Watervleit Arsenal. Never again would boats be grounded on the overslaugh.

The $600,000 spent for building and outfitting would have been considerably more if the engine from the burned-out *New World* had not been available. Everything about *St. John* was oversized. It took every ounce of steam from the seventy-six-inch cylinder to power the thirty buckets on each of the forty-foot wheels. At cruising speed, the thirty-ton walking beam seemed to take forever to traverse the fifteen feet of the cylinder stroke.

In 1863, it was the hands-down favorite night boat for the Saratoga Springs and Lake George crowd bound for another memorable season.

"Grandest Palace Drawing Room Steamers in the World—Drew and St. John of the People's Line Between New York and Albany." *Albany Institute of History and Art, Albany, New York.*

The grand saloon sported an elliptical roof with glittering gas chandeliers. Mirrors reflected costly bronzes imported from Paris and Rome displayed throughout the room. Passengers sat on solid rosewood chairs and settees covered in silk woven with flowers of a dozen hues. Those who didn't book one of the sumptuous cabins found the three hundred state rooms nearly as beautiful. They were reached by a carved staircase of Honduran mahogany. The twelve bridal rooms booked by happy couples on every trip were usually making Niagara Falls their destination.[83] *St. John*'s passengers were the people who dressed for dinner every night, had stiff card invitations on their mantle pieces and were on intimate speaking terms with the cream of society in New York and Newport. They were also the politically connected in Albany and Washington. So it was not unexpected to find the shipping page included a piece about the upcoming presidential election. Abraham Lincoln was seeking his second term. His Democratic opponent, Major General George B. McClellan, was a New Jersey favorite son expected to garner some extra votes locally:

> *Straw—The following vote was taken on the steamboat* St. John *[on] her trip from New York to Albany last evening: McClellan 119, Lincoln 43 This vote has been furnished us by a passenger on the boat who saw the vote taken and who is a reliable merchant of this city.*[84]

The deck of the *Monitor*. Isaac Newton, son of Isaac Newton, was its chief engineer and later was first engineer for the City of New York. *Rensselaer County Historical Society, Troy, New York.*

The war was creating young widows, many with small children. Shaker communities across the country welcomed these broken families by the hundreds to their communities. While some older boys went with their families, others were enrolled in one of a new generation of small private boarding schools. Composed of a few students and a couple of teachers, young men who once would have been marginally educated farmers or tradesmen now had the background to become a part of America's business and commercial future:

> *A Steamboat Incident—The Cadets (88 in number) of the school for the sons of deceased volunteers located at Suspension Bridge, came up from New York on the steamboat* St. John *last evening. There were a large number of passengers on board, who manifested great interest in their welfare. The Cadets went through an interesting drill and exercise in the presence of the passengers, and afterward a short speech was made by Col. Young who has charge of the school.*

*The speech was an appeal for aid for the institution, which depends upon voluntary contributions, and the handsome sum of $455 was contributed on the spot. Besides this, Mr. George C. Robbins of Portland, Oregon, gave to the Institution, and hearing one of the cadets from East Meridan N.Y. was called by the name of George Robbins, he adopted him and guaranteed to see to his education and treat him as his own child until he became of age—Mr. Dorking of Saratoga Springs also guaranteed to give $500 to be devoted to the special education and use of a cadet whom he selected from the rest. Mr. Merriman, from Rochester or Syracuse also gave $100. More speeches were made and the meeting finally closed by the singing of "Old Hundred."*[85]

One steamboat accident in southern waters found its way into the hands of a war weary readership. In the last weeks of conflict, the repatriation of soldiers from Confederate prisons had begun. Their living conditions had been barbaric. The newly incarcerated could only look forward to hunger, exposure and camp fever, as dysentery was called. Cholera and yellow fever from the plagues of mosquitoes further weakened prisoners, many with gross infections from untreated wounds. Among the worst, Camp Sumter in Andersonville, Georgia, was a stockade enclosure with a post and rail fence about nineteen feet within. Prisoners who climbed over the fence were shot on sight. It was called "the dead line."

Released on February 17, 1865, survivors were finally boarding *Sultana*, the largest steamboat in southern waters, for the next leg of their journey home. Filled to capacity, the decks were barely above the water line from an excess of human cargo. It exploded, killing more than 1,700. Of the nearly 2,200 on board, 1,976 were prisoners from Andersonville, Chickaman and Gettysburg who had managed to survive in the nearest place to hell on earth.

Judge W.D. Snow from Arkansas, a passenger aboard, reported the explosion happened about 3:00 a.m. The pilothouse and about one-third of the cabin roof fell in and was on fire, along with the boiler deck. He hoped to jump in the water to one side but found a sea of heads close together and the same on the other side. He observed husbands strapping wives and children into life jackets before slipping them over the rail to their fates. When the wheelhouse fell overboard, the boat turned in the river and everyone who had been safe in the bow from the flames were now in their full fury. The time between the explosion and the boat becoming a sheet of fire Judge Snow estimated at no more than twenty minutes.[86]

Later the same year, the catastrophe on board the *St. John* would be documented by reporters who happened to be at the dock the day of its

A steam dredge at the Troy dock, circa 1860. U.S. Army Corps of Engineers made the Hudson a priority because of the Watervleit Arsenal. *Rensselaer County Historical Society, Troy, New York.*

explosion. In 1846, S.A. Howland enlarged his book *Steamboat Disasters, Railroad Accidents, Shipwrecks*. He detailed forty-one of the most memorable steamboat catastrophes between the burning of *Phoenix* on September 5, 1819, and the sinking of the steam packet *Savannah* in a gale on November 22, 1841. His florid details were probably not histrionic, but they illustrated the dangers inherent in the new technology. Understanding, predicting and calculating stress and fatigue was just coming over the horizon. Until then, steamboat development might be compared to a series of scientific experiments on live subjects. Had Howland continued to write about steamboat disasters, the *St. John* would have held a place of honor in that book.[87]

At 6:00 a.m. on Sunday October 29, 1865, *St. John* was pulling into its pier. The paddle wheels were making thirteen revolutions per minute. The men in the boiler room had started to draw their fires, and the pressure was dropping from a running pressure of thirty pounds to between twenty and twenty-two. At the moment of the explosion, one fireman jumped overboard never to be seen again, and the other ran for the main deck. Some of the 275-degree water flooded the saloon deck, but most of it became a blast of scorching steam. The iron of the boiler was peeled back at least six feet, leaving a three-foot opening that looked as if it had been cut with a knife.

Most of the 110 passengers were still asleep in their cabins. A few were up early, dressed and on deck, watching the boat come into its mooring. The explosion from the port boiler room shook the vessel like an earthquake, throwing many from their berths, feet and bodies scalded. The skin of one child was lacerated and violently peeled away to leave raw marks of blood on boiled flesh. The features of the victims were not recognizable and described as bleached, mutilated, torn and livid by the force of the steam. Police closed off the pier. Assistance arrived, but too late for seven. Another seventeen were scalded. For some it was only their feet, and they were expected to live after a long convalescence. Five were badly scalded and died at the hospital.

The three staterooms nearest *St John*'s boiler simply vanished. As the impact went up, the hurricane deck was torn apart, making splinters that flew in all directions like miniature arrows. The gallery and compartments as far away as thirty feet were shattered and drenched with water. The large pillar in the center of the saloon was perforated by a piece of flying iron.

The living were quickly separated from the dead, who were covered with colorful silk quilts near the engine room bulkhead. Dry mattresses and blankets were laid astern for survivors. There were only 26 casualties among the 110 passengers. The wife and young daughter of Mr. Archambault, a distinguished member of the Canadian Parliament returning from Washington, lay alongside his body on the afterdeck surrounded by a number of traveling companions. An hour later, when all would have been out of their staterooms, the death toll would have been far greater. Two months earlier, when the boat would have been filled to capacity, the death toll could have been in the hundreds.

Reporters boarding the vessel soon after the explosion witnessed "hooligans stripping the victims of their rings, gold watches valued at $500, and wallets of cash." It was noted many of them were not yet dead. On the ceiling of the cabin nearest the explosion, one reporter witnessed seeing locks of human hair. Blood was spattered on the walls, a ladies' pocketbook burned out of recognition lay near earrings torn loose from their wearer's earlobes.[88] St. Luke's Church, where the marriage of Captain Fred Lyons and his bride took place a week before, was filled with the same people for the double funeral of the newlyweds who died on the last day of their honeymoon.

At least one survivor brought a suit against the New Jersey Steamboat Company amounting to $22,000 for pain and suffering incurred in the months following the accident. The jury upheld the award for $20,000 saying that "the defendants were common carriers and insured the lives of the passengers and also the vehicle used by them in their business. They were to see that everything appertaining to their business was manufactured in a perfect and effective manner so as to conduce the safety of the passengers; if the passengers are injured they are bound to make good."[89]

Jurisprudence had come of age since the explosion aboard *Reindeer*, which had been a similar scenario. In those days, the owners were individuals, not corporations, and not considered personally responsible for safe passage. Time after time, expert witnesses came forth to offer testimony weighted in the owners' favor. It was now no longer a "club of gentlemen" who owned the boat, but a business enterprise. Juries viewed the evidence more critically, seeking someone who could be held accountable. The first draft of a bill of rights for passengers was finally being written:

> *In the Supreme Court today before Judge Cordosa, a verdict was rendered against the New Jersey Steamboat Company in favor of Nathan C.*

Stateroom saloon of *Berkshire* (1860–1864), which burned. It was a sister ship to the popular *St. John. New York State Archives, Albany, New York.*

*Caldwell for twenty thousand dollars. Mr. C sued for damages sustained by the explosion of the boilers of the steamboat* St. John *belonging to that Company. The verdict is the heaviest that has been given to a similar case for many years.*[90]

*As deadly as the steamboat was, its dangers turned out to be the catalyst to compel Congress to consider the role of government in private affairs on behalf of an outraged and fearful public. The result was [that] Congress came to terms with the realities of technological progress and worked through the various Constitutional issues associated with government regulation. A foundation for the current network of administrative agencies that protect the welfare of Americans was laid. Every time someone buys a candy bar or takes an aspirin or purchases stock or flies in an airplane, there is a federal regulatory agency behind the scenes ensuring the safety and welfare of that individual. It is because of the efforts to prevent steamboat-boiler explosions in the nineteenth century that individuals today no longer entrust their lives to chance, but to the federal government.*[91]

Rebuilt and refitted, "the new *St. John*" was back on the river in time for the high season the following year. On every trip, the crowded river around Kingston always tested the skills of steamboat pilots. Schooners carrying lumber from Watervleit and secured by thick hawsers behind the largest towboats passed through on their way to the mouth of the Hudson. There, they would be set loose like big brown birds with white wings. At the eastern terminal of the Delaware and Hudson Barge Canal coal depot, a number of steamers were assembling tows of up to eighty barges. Some would be going north to the capital district, but many were headed for docks around New York. In the vicinity, there were always outbound schooners sailing under their own power, weighed down with coal slated for New England coastal towns. Slow moving and subject to the vagaries of the wind, they had the right of way. Through this mêlée, the *St. John* with its great wheels turning about fifteen times a minute would pass through at optimum speed. Even at night when there were only a few boats on the river, there was always a chance their paths would cross:

*The "Rondout Freeman" says that on Saturday morning about two o'clock as the schooner* A.W. Ellis *was bound down the river above Poughkeepsie, she tacked straight across the river. Just then the steamboat* St. John *overtook her and in attempting to pass struck her near the fore chains staving in her bulwarks and railing. It seems the schooner was under the west shore when she tacked and the pilot of the* St. John *intended to pass between her and the shore, but on nearing her he was deceived by the shadow of the land and thinking there was not room enough hauled to the eastward intending to run across her bow with the result as stated. No blame is attached to Capt Ferguson of the schooner. The damage was about $500 and is being repaired at the docks of McCausland in this city. The vessel is from Belfast Me. and started from Rondout on Friday with a load of coal.*[92]

The New York papers regularly ran a filler simply called "Collisions in the Harbor," reporting on the fender benders of the previous twenty-four hours. In a crowded harbor, large steamboats like *St. John* had to navigate the small tugboats nicknamed, "the mosquito fleet." In such cases, neither party owned up to the blame, and the tug pilots accepted response was, "I didn't hear the whistle." By the time the great boat came to a stop, the tug would have rammed it below the guards, sometimes wiping out a few of the paddles in the collision. The tugs tended to have more damage done to them, in the range of $400 to $600. The thick white oak planks and ribs cut from trees sometimes three hundred years old made the steamer's hull impervious to such minor assaults.

While there was little that could be done about overcrowding, some progress was finally being made in preventing nighttime accidents. Powerful Drummond Lights using gas or versions of lighthouse beacons with lenses, reflectors and oil lamps could have inspired a spotlight for steamboats decades earlier, but it never happened. Electricity and the carbon arc light were the triggers. A feature called "Electric Headlights for Ships" promised an end to nighttime collisions. A demonstration for an intense light to be used aboard vessels was conducted aboard the *City of Columbus.* The experiment created a mist through which the pencil like beam was shone. Objects three miles from the pier were seen in high relief, and the direction vessels were moving could be ascertained. Any lights on board the vessels remained clearly visible as well. The principal objection to electric lights had been that the light would be reflected back in the operator's eyes. This was proven untrue.[93]

Though racing was officially banned from the river in the 1850s, some heated time trials continued over the years. Anticipating an official blind eye would be turned, sometimes the event was thrilling enough for a paper to report it as "local color." The Newburgh paper the following morning printed a detailed account of events from the night before. This account may have been the last of the great steamboat races when it was remembered in 1909 by Charles Hallenbeck, one of the best historians of the Hudson River steamboats.

*St. John*, *City of Catskill* and *Saratoga* were the night boats on November 8, 1881. An extra thick fog delayed their departures from New York by several hours. Even pilots with decades on the river waited them out. When it eventually lifted, all three left their respective docks. Entering the river, a race began. Even though it was considerably larger and heavier than the other two, *St. John* was favored:

> *Considerable interest was excited along the river front at one o'clock when the night boats* St. John, *City of Catskill* and *Saratoga passed this city at racing speed. Smoke was pouring out of their stacks, their wheels were churning the water into a foam and leaving long heavy swells behind them. Boatmen sought favorable points of observation and waved their hats at the contesting steamboats. When they came through the Highlands, the* St. John *was leading and the* City of Catskill *was last, but off the Pennsylvania coal dock the* City *passed the* Saratoga *and off the long dock was several lengths ahead. The* St. John *was about a quarter of a mile ahead at the time and was sailing fast. The* St. John *has always been considered the fastest of the "big" night boats and the way she kept ahead of the smaller boats was greatly to her credit.*
>
> *The* City of Catskill, *however, overhauled her larger rival before Poughkeepsie was reached, passing that place about one and a half minutes ahead of the* St. John *while the* Saratoga *was eight minutes behind.*[94]

The older boat continued to be a favorite, refreshed every season but never extensively redecorated. After twenty years of service, it was old fashioned, and its 1860s opulence became part of its charm. The extensive descriptions of weddings on the social pages often closed with "the happy couple will leave for Niagara Falls this afternoon on the *St. John*." It had been Captain St. John's last command. He was a man of tireless energy, the general manager, superintendent and treasurer of the People's Line and, with Daniel Drew, the last of the original directors. During the season, everyone knew he would be found on the river. His first wheel had been the *Westchester* in 1834. From there, he went on to be the first to command the premier steamers: *Emerald*, *Rochester*, *Charter Oak*, *Hendrick Hudson*, *Knickerbocker*, *Oregon* and *New World*.

In 1875, at seventy-five, he was still putting the interests of the steamboats first. He would spend some hours in the headquarter offices on Fulton Street and then conclude each day overseeing the work aboard the boat that bore his name. His fellow directors of the People's Line had been of a mind to sell it, giving as evidence the wear and tear on the structure and mechanicals. New carpets, furniture and a coat of paint—what the public saw—was an insignificant outlay by comparison. More than $40,000 would be needed to return it to first-class condition. Offers by businesses that would run it as an excursion boat for a few years before scrapping had been received and were being considered. St. John did not want it sold, but he was well aware of the cost of the refurbishment.

On Friday, April 23, he visited the dock at the foot of East Nineteenth Street for the last time. One can imagine his making a thorough inspection of the progress on the structure, mechanicals and passenger accommodations, taking time to talk with everyone he saw. They had worked together for many years.

His last stop was the barbershop. There he had set up a cot and brought in a comfortable chair from which he would often be aroused at the end of the day. He was finally alone. Taking a small revolver from his pocket, he put a bullet through his right temple.[95] The boat was not sold or sent to the breakers but went on another decade, remaining the all-time favorite of the Hudson River steamboats.

The Saturday evening papers on January 24, 1885, carried the headline no one wanted to read: "The *St. John* Burned—One of the Floating Palaces of the Hudson in Flames." That morning, the sun rose on a blackened wreck at Pier 41 Canal Street, sunk to the top of the guards by the weight of the water pumped on it. The fire broke out shortly after 3:00 a.m. that morning. Fire apparatus had been hindered arriving at other fires throughout the last two days by a heavy snowfall, which made most streets impassible. That did not hinder the Debrosses Street Ferry fire brigade, which was soon on the scene. The two harbor fireboats appeared promptly to the telegraph alarm sent from the Debrosses Street station. About a dozen tugs also swarmed around, spraying their hoses for the next two hours. It appeared that the fire started in the foredeck area, but no cause had been determined by press time. In his interview, the captain said that part of the boat had just received a fresh coat of paint. An unidentified photograph of the day showing a stateroom hall is probably the *St. John*. This picture would have been taken of the other end of the boat from the fire and explains its pristine freshness. While documenting a catastrophe, it also documents the grand splendor of these boats.[96]

Estimated value of the boat before the fire was $700,000, of which $200,000 was covered by fire insurance. About $5,000 had just been spent

Dock wagons at Steamboat Square, circa 1918. This dock can be seen in the background of the pre-1875 "Sunnyside" photograph. *Albany Institute of History and Art, Albany, New York.*

on new timbers around the engine, which was now worthless because of the intense heat. The boat named for a captain who never had an accident was towed from its mooring a few weeks later. In the spring, *Dean Richmond* assumed its place on the river, but not in the hearts of the traveling public.

Paddle-wheel steamboats with great walking beam engines continued to be built for the "Hudson River Day Line" into the twentieth century. A new *Hendrick Hudson* launched in 1906 was the first with a $1 million price tag. The *Robert Fulton* arrived on the river in time to take part in the centennial ceremonies marking Robert Fulton's first trip up the Hudson. In that ceremony was the towboat *Norwich*, built in 1836 and in service until 1917. It had the honor of towing a replica of Henry Hudson's 1609 *Half Moon*, given to the people of the United States by the Dutch government.

The *Washington Irving* followed in 1912 and the *Alexander Hamilton* in 1924. One can experience a trip on this boat by checking out the You Tube video "A glorious Hudson River Steamboat called the Alexander Hamilton." When the *Peter Stuyvesant*, last of the steamers, was built in 1927, the public was no

Captain Samuel Schuyler near Newburgh, with Stormking in the distance, remembering his sixty-eight years on the river. *Schuyler Collection, New York State Archives, Albany, New York.*

longer dependent on the boats for transportation. Newspapers referred to the company as "the Red Line." They were exotic excursion boats more than working boats, and no longer floating printing presses turning out profits for the company. It was no surprise when the papers announced that September 13, 1948, would be the last trip for the *Robert Fulton* from Albany to New York City.

Today, the Albany waterfront—with its rows of warehouses, the basin where boats were moored and the dock crowded with passengers—has been filled in, paved over and forgotten. The Erie Canal, once an artery of commerce for the Northeast, is part of a public authority and almost all the boats on it are for recreational use. When James Schuyler photographed his father at one of the steamboat docks in 1881, it was a Sunday afternoon when no boats were running. Now, the Hudson looks like that almost every day.

# NOTES

## Chapter 1

1. Charles A. Hallenbeck, "Annals of the Hudson River," 1807–1907, State Library Archives, Albany, NY, file 1828.
2. Ibid.
3. Letter of condolence, Mrs. Finche, Swallow disaster, New York State Archives, Albany, NY.

## Chapter 2

4. *Mercantile Advertiser*, "Explosion of the Steamboat Aetna," May 17, 1824.
5. Hallenbeck, "Annals," file 1824.
6. *Evening Post*, "The Steamboat Henry Eckford Arrived," May 26, 1824.
7. *Spectator*, "Steamship Benjamin Franklin," September 2, 1824.
8. Hallenbeck, "Annals," file 1824.
9. *Republican Telegraph.* "The destruction of lives," May 26, 1824.
10. *Evening Post*, "For Philadelphia—,"February 10, 1826.
11. Ibid., "Fastest Boat in the World," June 4, 1835.
12. *Cabinet*, "It Is Stated in Some Accounts—," January 21, 1840.

# CHAPTER 3

13. F. Van Loon Ryder, "Old Timers Boats of the Hudson River," *Greene County (NY) News*, February 17, 1966.
14. *New York Tribune*, "Mr. Fellows, steward of the Rip Van Winkle," May 21,1849.
15. *Daily (Utica) Observer*, "The Sinking of the Empire—Deplorable Calamity," May 19, 1849.
16. *New York Tribune*, "Disaster on the Hudson—Statement of Mr. Burden," May 22, 1849.
17. Ibid., "Empire of Troy Sinks," June 6, 1849.
18. *Evening Journal*, "New York Albany & Troy Steamboat Line," April 15, 1843.

# CHAPTER 4

19. Ibid., "The Masses in Motion—," September 17, 1847.
20. *New York Herald*, "Court Docket," August 23, 1847.
21. Ibid., "Steamboat Ashore," November 14, 1848.
22. *Evening Post*, "Robbery Onboard the Steamboat Niagara," August 25, 1850.
23. *Daily Freeman*, "During the Fog of Yesterday Morning—," September 25, 1879.

# CHAPTER 5

24. *Evening Post*, "Exhibition of Splendid Furniture," August 2, 1843.
25. *Evening Journal*, "Just Received—," October 30, 1843.
26. *New York Tribune*, "Summer Travel—Saratoga Is Full to Overflowing," August 16, 1843.
27. George W. Murdock, "Lexington," *Daily Freeman*, February 1, 1938.
28. *New York Herald*, "Arrival of the Ninety-first Regiment," December 22, 1861.
29. Ibid., "The Battle at Mumfordsville," ibid.

# CHAPTER 6

30. Preble, *Chronological History*, 206–7.

31. *Greene County (NY) News*, May 13, 1965.

32. *New York Daily*, "Sale of Steamer Property—," September 19,1874.

# CHAPTER 7

33. *Sabbath Recorder*, "The New Steamboat *Isaac Newton*," June 25, 1846.

34. Browder, "Steamboat Wars," April 28, 2013.

35. *Evening Journal*, "The River," December 14, 1847.

36. Ibid., "Hungarian Exiles," November 1, 1848.

37. *Evening Post*, "Court Docket," September 24, 1853.

38. *Observer*, "By Magnetic Telegraph—The Steamboat *Isaac Newton*," April 2, 1857.

39. *Evening Express*, "The Steamboat *Isaac Newton* is on Castleton Bar," December 24, 1861.

40. *Daily Palladium*, "Destruction of the Isaac Newton," December 7, 1863.

41. *Daily Courier*, "The New Steamer New World," June 4,1849.

42. Ibid., "Steamer *New World*—12 O'clock," October 29, 1859.

43. *Evening Post*, "*New World* Sinks," October 27, 1859.

44. Ibid.

45. *Evening Journal*, The Steamer *New World* Is Up to Her Guards," July 5, 1861.

46. *Morning Herald*, "It is Stated," February 13, 1863.

47. *State League of Temperance and Freedom*, "The Steamer *New World*," June 11, 1864.

# CHAPTER 8

48. Huntington, *Zythara*, "Rail Road Chorus," 26.

49. *Albany Statesman*, "Millard Fillmore," June 30, 1856.

50. *Daily Tribune*, "The Japanese Bills," September 7, 1860.

51. *Daily (Poughkeepsie) Eagle*, "End of the Steamer Alida," September 26, 1883.

52. *Daily Tribune*, "The New Steamboat *Francis Skiddy* to Run as a Day Boat," June 12, 1852.

53. *Express*, "Boats Held at Castleton," March 3, 1857.

54. *Daily Whig*, "The Courier and Enquirer Has the Following Paragraph," July 1, 1855.
55. *Hartford Calendar*, "Steamboat *Francis Skiddy* Sinks Sloop," October 23, 1852.
56. George W. Murdock, *"Francis Skiddy," Daily Freeman*, February 22, 1938.

## CHAPTER 9

57. *Western New Yorker*, "Discoveries of a Half Century from the Scientific American," June 3, 1851.
58. Ibid., "Great Speed—," May 1, 1851.
59. *Daily Tribune*, "The Trip of the Steamboat *Reindeer*," August 28, 1850.
60. *Daily (Brooklyn) Eagle*, "The New Steamer *Reindeer*," August 29, 1850.
61. *Daily Courier*, "Barrytown, May 6, 1851—," May 8, 1851.
62. *Daily Standard*, "Another Steamboat Accident on the Hudson—," September 7, 1852.
63. *Daily Courier*, "Steamboat *Reindeer* Fire," September 7, 1852.
64. *Daily Star*, "Hudson River *Reindeer* Explosion—," September 7, 1852.
65. *Daily Tribune*, "The Reindeer Explosion—Official Verdict of Coroner's Jury—," September 9,1852 .
66. *New York Herald*, "The Steamboat Calamities—Indictments—," October 1, 1852.
67. *New York Tribune*, "Reindeer Explosion-Further Particulars," September 7,1852.
68. *Daily Tribune*, "Court Docket—The Steamboat *Reindeer*," January 22, 1853.
69. Ibid.
70. *Evening Journal*, "Indictment Steamboat *Reindeer*," January 22, 1853.

## CHAPTER 10

71. *Greene County (NY) News*, February 27,1964, March 5, 1964.
72. Kalafus, "Henry Clay."
73. *Greene County (NY) News*, January 27, 1966.
74. Ibid.
75. Kalafus, "Henry Clay."
76. Ibid.

# CHAPTER 11

77. *Northern Christian Advocate*, "Shipping News," March 29, 1848.
78. *Daily Times*, "Steamboat Daniel Drew," September 13, 1876.
79. *Daily Freeman*, "The Day Line Steamboat *Daniel Drew*—," June 14, 1879.
80. *Evening Register*, "Steamboat *Daniel Drew* Burned," September 1, 1886.
81. *Daily Journal*, "Sea Serpent in the Hudson," September 3, 1886.
82. *Evening Register*, "Passing on the Steamer Drew," June 16, 1901.

# CHAPTER 12

83. *World*, "The New Steamboat *St. John*," March 15,1864.
84. *Daily (Utica) Observer*, "Straw—," September 13, 1863.
85. Ibid., "A Steamboat Incident—," September 13, 1863.
86. *Madison Observer*, "Explosion Aboard Steamboat *Sultana*," May 10, 1865.
87. Howland, 50–284.
88. *World*, "St John Explosion," October 31, 1865; *Sun*, October 30, 1865.
89. *Daily Tribune*, "Steamboat Company Found Liable," April 19, 1870.
90. *Daily Evening Star*, "In the Supreme Court Today," May 28, 1868.
91. Sandukas, "Gently Down the Stream."
92. *Daily (Poughkeepsie) Eagle*, "Steamboat Collision," September 29, 1873.
93. *New York Herald*, "Electric Headlights for Ships," June 16, 1880.
94. C.A. Hollenbeck, "River Races Mild in the Last 25 Years," *Evening Post*, September 25, 1909.
95. *Daily Tribune*, "Suicide of Alanson P. St. John," April 24, 1875,
96. *Evening Journal*, "The *St. John* Burned—," January 24, 1885.

# BIBLIOGRAPHY

## BOOKS

Buckman, David Lear. *Old Steamboat Days on the Hudson River*. New York: Grafton Press, 1907.

Dunwell, Frances F. *The Hudson River Highlands*. New York: Columbia University Press, 1991.

Gerber, Morris. *Old Albany*. 4 vols. Saratoga Springs, NY: Portofino Publishing, 1987.

Hamilton, Captain John G. *Hudson River Pilot: From Steamboats to Super Tanker*. Hensonville, NY: Black Dome Press, 2001.

Hunt, Gaillard. *As We Were: Life in America 1814*. Stockbridge, MA: Berkshire House Publishers, 1993.

Huntington, F.L. *The Zythara*. New York: Mason Brothers, 1854: 26.

Larkin, Jack. *The Reshaping of Every Day Life 1790–1840*. New York: Harper & Row, 1988.

Lewis, Tom. *The Hudson: A History*. New Haven, CT: Yale University Press, 2005.

McEneny, John J. *Albany: Capital City on the Hudson*. Albany, NY: Albany Institute of History and Art, 1981.

Morrison, John H. *History of American Steam Navigation*. New York: Wm F. Sametz and Co., 1909.

Preble, George Henry. *A Chronological History of the Origin and Development of Steam Navigation*. 2nd ed. Philadelphia PA: L.R. Hamersley & Co ,1895.

Ringwald, Donald C. *Hudson River Day Line*. New York: Fordham University Press, 1990.

———. *Steamboats for Rondout*. Providence, RI: Steamship Historical Society of America, 1981.

Stanton, Samuel Ward. *American Steam Vessels*. New York: Smith and Stanton, 1895.

Tantillo, Len. *Visions of New York State: The Historical Paintings of L.F. Tantillo*. Wappingers Falls, NY: Shawangunk Press, 1996.

Weymouth, Lally. *America in 1876: The Way We Were*. New York: Random House, Vintage Books, 1976.

Whittier, Bob. *Paddle Wheel Steamers and the Giant Engines*. Duxbury, MA: Seamaster Inc., 1987.

Young, John H. *Our Deportment: Manners Conduct and Dress of the Most Refined Society; Compiled from the Latest Reliable Authorities*. Detroit MI: F.B. Dickerson & Co., 1881.

# PERIODICALS

Blackburn, Roderic H., and William P. Palmer. "Hudson River Steamboats in Prints an Paintings." *Columbia County History and Heritage* (Spring 2005): 30–5.

Eyre, Jim. "The *Henry Clay* vs. the *Armenia*: A Fatal Steamboat Race." *Columbia County History and Heritage* (Spring 2005): 26–7.

Lizzi, Dominic. "The Swallow House." *Columbia County History and Heritage* (Spring 2005): 38–9.

Murdock, George W. "Hudson River Steamboats." Column in *Kingston (NY) Daily Freeman*, December 1937–August 1941.

Schram, Margaret. "Hudson: The River Seaport." *Columbia County History and Heritage* (Spring 2005): 11–15.

# UNPUBLISHED MANUSCRIPT

Hallenbeck, Charles. "Annals of the Hudson River 1807–1908." Manuscript files for unpublished book, New York State Archives, Albany, New York.

# Newspapers Online

Albany Statesman, Albany, New York.
Cabinet, Schenectady, New York.
Daily Courier, Buffalo, New York.
Daily Eagle, Brooklyn, New York.
Daily Eagle, Poughkeepsie, New York.
Daily Evening Star, Schenectady, New York.
Daily Freeman, Kingston, New York .
Daily Journal, Syracuse, New York.
Daily Observer, Utica, New York.
Daily Observer, New York.
Daily Palladium, Oswego, New York.
Daily Standard, Syracuse, New York.
Daily Star, New York.
Daily Times, Oswego, New York.
Daily Tribune, New York.
Daily Whig, Troy New York.
Democrat, Skaneateles, New York.
Evening Express, New York.
Evening Journal, Albany, New York.
Evening Post, New York.
Evening Register, Hudson, New York.
Express, New York.
Greene County News, Hudson, New York.
Hartford Calendar, Hartford, Connecticut.
Madison Observer, Morrisville, New York.
Mercantile Advertiser, New York.
Morning Herald, Utica, New York.
New York Daily.
New York Herald.
New York Tribune.
Northern Christian Advocate, Auburn, New York.
Observer, Madison, New York.
Republican Telegraph, Poughkeepsie, New York.
Sabbath Recorder, New York.
Spectator, New York.
State League of Temperance and Freedom, Syracuse, New York.
Sun, New York.
Western New Yorker, Warsaw, New York.
World, New York.

# INTERNET

Browder, Clifford. "Steamboat Wars on the Hudson." No Place for Normal, April 28, 2013. cbrowder.blogspot.com/...teamboat-wars-on-hudson. html.

Howland, S. A. (Southworth Allen). *Steamboat Disasters, Railroad Accidents, Shipwrecks.* Worcester, MA: W. Lazell, 1843. http://archive.org/details/ steamboatdisaste01howl.

Kalafus, Jim. "Henry Clay, 19[th] Century General Slocum." September 4, 2005. www.encyclopedia-titanica.org.

Ryder, F. Van Loon. "Old Timers' Boats of the Hudson River." February 17, 1966. mhttp//www.rootsweb.ancestry.com/nygreen2/old_timers_-_boats_of_the_hudson.htm.

Sandukas, Gregory P. "Gently Down the Stream: How Exploding Steamboat Boilers in the 19[th] Century Ignited Federal Public Welfare Regulation." Third year paper, Harvard Law School, April 30, 2002.

# INDEX

# ABOUT THE AUTHOR

For my tenth birthday, my parents gave me a Kodak Flash 20 camera. The first twenty pictures included a clock with wooden works, a tombstone indicating the deceased died of smallpox and a chair in which General Lafayette sat in 1824. He was waiting for the coach horses to be changed on his way to Albany, having just visited his Revolutionary War friend General Benjamin Tallmadge in neighboring Litchfield. The resulting opaque projector program, "Once Upon a Time in Goshen," was the first of nearly fifty illustrated talks I have given because I enjoy hands-on history. They have been the one continuous thread running through my career from secondary English Teacher to United Church of Christ minister and concluding as a family therapist in an alcoholism treatment program.

Renovating a house built by Captain Samuel Schuyler for his daughter began my interest in his life, the steamboats and the waterfront that is now filled in, paved over and forgotten. Old newspapers and photographs from when the river was humming with activity inspired more talks and, finally, the first of what I hope will be three books on this subject.

.